Weather and Climate Inventory
National Park Service
Sierra Nevada Network

Natural Resource Technical Report NPS/SIEN/NRTR—2007/042
WRCC Report 2007-17

Christopher A. Davey, Kelly T. Redmond, and David B. Simeral
Western Regional Climate Center
Desert Research Institute
2215 Raggio Parkway
Reno, Nevada 89512-1095

June 2007

U.S. Department of the Interior
National Park Service
Natural Resource Program Center
Fort Collins, Colorado

The Natural Resource Publication series addresses natural resource topics that are of interest and applicability to a broad readership in the National Park Service and to others in the management of natural resources, including the scientific community, the public, and the National Park Service conservation and environmental constituencies. Manuscripts are peer-reviewed to ensure that the information is scientifically credible, technically accurate, appropriately written for the intended audience, and designed and published in a professional manner.

The Natural Resources Technical Reports series is used to disseminate the peer-reviewed results of scientific studies in the physical, biological, and social sciences for both the advancement of science and the achievement of the National Park Service mission. The reports provide contributors with a forum for displaying comprehensive data that are often deleted from journals because of page limitations. Current examples of such reports include the results of research that address natural resource management issues; natural resource inventory and monitoring activities; resource assessment reports; scientific literature reviews; and peer-reviewed proceedings of technical workshops, conferences, or symposia.

Views and conclusions in this report are those of the authors and do not necessarily reflect policies of the National Park Service. Mention of trade names or commercial products does not constitute endorsement or recommendation for use by the National Park Service.

Printed copies of reports in these series may be produced in a limited quantity and they are only available as long as the supply lasts. This report is also available from the Natural Resource Publications Management website (http://www.nature.nps.gov/publications/NRPM) on the Internet or by sending a request to the address on the back cover.

Please cite this publication as follows:

Davey, C. A., K. T. Redmond, and D. B. Simeral. 2007. Weather and Climate Inventory, National Park Service, Sierra Nevada Network. Natural Resource Technical Report NPS/SIEN/NRTR—2007/042. National Park Service, Fort Collins, Colorado.

NPS/SIEN/NRTR—2007/042, June 2007

Contents

Contents (continued)

Figures

Tables

Appendixes

Acronyms

AASC	American Association of State Climatologists
ACIS	Applied Climate Information System
ASOS	Automated Surface Observing System
AWOS	Automated Weather Observing System
BAMI	Bay Area Mesoscale Initiative
BLM	Bureau of Land Management
CARB	California Air Resources Board
CASTNet	Clean Air Status and Trends Network
CDEC	California Data Exchange Center
CDWR	California Department of Water Resources
CIMIS	California Irrigation Management Information System
COOP	Cooperative Observer Program
CRN	Climate Reference Network
CRREL	Cold Regions Research and Engineering Laboratory
CSS	California Cooperative Snow Survey
CWOP	Citizen Weather Observer Program
DEPO	Devils Postpile National Monument
DFIR	Double-Fence Intercomparison Reference
DRI	Desert Research Institute
DST	daylight savings time
ENSO	El Niño Southern Oscillation
EPA	Environmental Protection Agency
FAA	Federal Aviation Administration
FIPS	Federal Information Processing Standards
GMT	Greenwich Mean Time
GOES	Geostationary Operational Environmental Satellite
GPMP	NPS Gaseous Pollutant Monitoring Program
GPS	Global Positioning System
I&M	NPS Inventory and Monitoring Program
LST	local standard time
NADP	National Atmospheric Deposition Program
NASA	National Aeronautics and Space Administration
NCDC	National Climatic Data Center
NetCDF	Network Common Data Form
NOAA	National Oceanic and Atmospheric Administration
NPS	National Park Service
NRCS	Natural Resources Conservation Service
NRCS-SC	NRCS snowcourse network
NWS	National Weather Service
PDO	Pacific Decadal Oscillation
PNA	Pacific-North America Oscillation
POMS	Portable Ozone Monitoring System
PRISM	Parameter Regression on Independent Slopes Model
RAWS	Remote Automated Weather Station network

RCC	regional climate center
SAO	Surface Airways Observation network
SEKI	Sequoia and Kings Canyon National Parks
SIEN	Sierra Nevada Inventory and Monitoring Network
SOD	Summary Of the Day
Surfrad	Surface Radiation Budget network
SNOTEL	Snowfall Telemetry network
UCSB	University of California Santa Barbara
USACE	U.S. Army Corps of Engineers
USDA	U.S. Department of Agriculture
USGS	U.S. Geological Survey
UTC	Coordinated Universal Time
WBAN	Weather Bureau Army Navy
WMO	World Meteorological Organization
WRCC	Western Regional Climate Center
WX4U	Weather For You network
YOSE	Yosemite National Park

Executive Summary

Climate is a dominant factor driving the physical and ecological processes affecting Sierra Nevada Network (SIEN) park units. Topographical influences are instrumental in defining the climate of the SIEN. Low to mid-elevations have a Mediterranean-type climate, with hot, dry summers and cool, wet winters. Higher elevations are dominated by much cooler conditions, with abundant snowfall. Much less precipitation falls east of the Sierra crest due to rainshadowing effects. Global-scale climate changes are already impacting SIEN ecosystems, including shifted plant growth cycles and streamflow peaks due to snowmelt. Global warming is likely to shift habitats to higher elevations in the SIEN. Some species may not adjust to these changes as readily, leading to a decline in species diversity. Increasing temperatures and more frequent droughts would affect fire regimes and pest/disease outbreaks. Because of its influence on the ecology of SIEN park units, climate was identified as a high-priority vital sign for SIEN and is one of the 12 basic inventories to be completed for all National Park Service (NPS) Inventory and Monitoring Program (I&M) networks.

This project was initiated to inventory past and present climate monitoring efforts in the SIEN. In this report, we provide the following information:

- Overview of broad-scale climatic factors and zones important to SIEN park units.
- Inventory of weather and climate station locations in and near SIEN park units relevant to the NPS I&M Program.
- Results of an inventory of metadata on each weather station, including affiliations for weather-monitoring networks, types of measurements recorded at these stations, and information about the actual measurements (length of record, etc.).
- Initial evaluation of the adequacy of coverage for existing weather stations and recommendations for improvements in monitoring weather and climate.

Extremely rugged topography and the orientation of the Sierra Nevada with respect to incoming storms both help to create severe climatic gradients in SIEN park units. Mean annual precipitation is highest in the northernmost portions of Yosemite National Park (YOSE), which generally exceed 1400 mm each year. The driest locations in the SIEN occur in southeastern Sequoia and Kings Canyon National Parks (SEKI), where portions of the Kern River valley receive less than 600 mm on average each year. Mean annual temperatures across the SIEN are warmest in western portions of both SEKI and YOSE (around 0°C), and coolest in the highest elevations of SEKI (below -3°C). Topographical influences are also quite significant for both winter and summer temperatures in the SIEN. January minimum temperatures generally get below -18°C in the highest elevations of SEKI, while the lowest elevations of both SEKI and YOSE easily exceed 30°C in July. The El Niño Southern Oscillation (ENSO), Pacific Decadal Oscillation (PDO), and Pacific-North America Oscillation (PNA) all influence intra- and inter-annual climate variability in the SIEN.

Through a search of national databases and inquiries to NPS staff, we have identified 98 weather and climate stations within SIEN park units. The most stations within park boundaries were found in SEKI (55). To date, we have identified 49 active stations within network boundaries (26 in SEKI, 22 in YOSE, and one in Devils Postpile National Monument).

The stations identified within SEKI and YOSE are generally located along primary roadways or near visitor centers and other high-traffic areas. Many of these stations are also no longer active, resulting in a relatively small number of long-term climate records. Only six active stations within SIEN park units have observation records of 50 years or longer. Existing stations that have long-term records are valuable for climate-monitoring efforts and will hopefully be encouraged to continue operating. In the more remote areas of both SEKI and YOSE, the primary sources of weather data come from California Cooperative Snow Survey (CSS) sites. It is therefore beneficial for climate monitoring efforts in the SIEN that the NPS encourage the continued operation of these sites as well as the addition of new sites. Other research groups are making valuable measurements of weather and climate elements within SIEN parks. Examples of such research groups are the University of Washington, the Scripps Institution of Oceanography, and the University of California, Santa Barbara.

With most of the weather and climate stations within YOSE being located along the main roadways (e.g., Tioga Road) or in areas such as Yosemite Village, significant tracts of land within the park unit remain unsampled, primarily in northeastern and southeastern YOSE. These areas are quite remote, with very difficult access. However, the overall understanding of the spatial characteristics of weather and climate patterns in YOSE would benefit greatly if weather and climate data could be obtained from these unsampled locations. One suitable strategy might be to install CSS stations in these areas. Many of the existing CSS sites in YOSE are also located in remote locations similar to the unsampled areas in YOSE.

Few of the active weather and climate stations in SEKI sample conditions at higher elevations, which occur primarily in the eastern portions of SEKI. Like YOSE, the remoteness of eastern portions of SEKI makes it difficult to install and maintain the stations that are needed to better sample the spatial characteristics of weather and climate within SEKI. Additional analyses could be conducted to evaluate the need for (and locations for) additional high-elevation sites. The Remote Automated Weather Station (RAWS) site "Rattlesnake" is the only RAWS station in eastern SEKI and it only takes observations during the summer. The NPS may want to consider expanding operations at this site in order to include fall, winter, and spring observations. Unfortunately, several long-term stations in and near SEKI appear to have ceased taking measurements within the last couple of years. Each of these records can provide valuable climate information for SEKI. We recommend that the NPS consider re-activating those recently-ended sites that are within SEKI. For those stations outside of SEKI, it would be beneficial for NPS to work with the local persons or agencies responsible for maintaining these long-term sites and encourage them to resume measurements at these valuable climate stations.

Acknowledgements

This work was supported and completed under Task Agreement H8R07010001, with the Great Basin Cooperative Ecosystem Studies Unit. We would like to acknowledge very helpful assistance from various National Park Service personnel associated with the Sierra Nevada Inventory and Monitoring Network. Particular thanks are extended to Linda Mutch and Andi Heard. We want to thank the various SIEN park staff that assisted in compiling station metadata, including Georgia Dempsey, Deanna Dulen, Annie Esperanza, Bob Meadows, Jim Roche, Nate Stephenson, Jan Van Wagtendonk, and Katy Warner. We also thank John Gross, Margaret Beer, Grant Kelly, and Greg McCurdy for all their help. Portions of the work were supported by the NOAA Western Regional Climate Center.

1.0. Introduction

Weather and climate are key drivers in ecosystem structure and function. Global- and regional-scale climate variations have a tremendous impact on natural systems (Chapin et al. 1996; Schlesinger 1997; Jacobson et al. 2000; Bonan 2002). Long-term patterns in temperature and precipitation provide first-order constraints on potential ecosystem structure and function. Secondary constraints are realized from the intensity and duration of individual weather events and, additionally, from seasonality and inter-annual climate variability. These constraints influence the fundamental properties of ecologic systems, such as soil–water relationships, plant–soil processes, and nutrient cycling, as well as disturbance rates and intensity. These properties, in turn, influence the life-history strategies supported by a climate regime (Neilson 1987; Rodriguez-Iturbe 2000; Mutch et al. 2005).

Given the importance of climate, it is one of 12 basic inventories to be completed by the National Park Service (NPS) Inventory and Monitoring Program (I&M) network (I&M 2006). The purpose of the NPS I&M is to develop and provide scientifically sound information on the current status and long term trends in the composition, structure, and function of park ecosystems, and to determine how well current management practices are sustaining those ecosystems. This is accomplished through park-wide inventories and a long-term monitoring program. In establishing a service-wide natural resources inventory and monitoring program, the NPS created networks of parks that are linked by geography and shared natural resource characteristics. Working within networks improves the efficiency of inventory and monitoring because parks are able to share budgets, staffing, and other resources to plan and implement an integrated program. The Sierra Nevada Network (SIEN) includes four NPS units: Devils Postpile National Monument (DEPO), Sequoia and Kings Canyon National Parks (SEKI)—two distinct parks managed as one unit, and Yosemite National Park (YOSE) (Table 1.1; Figure 1.1)

Table 1.1. Park units in the Sierra Nevada Network.

Acronym	Name
DEPO	Devils Postpile National Monument
SEKI	Sequoia and Kings Canyon National Parks
YOSE	Yosemite National Park

As primary environmental drivers for the other vital signs, weather and climate patterns present various practical and management consequences and implications for the NPS (Oakley et al. 2003). Most park units observe weather and climate elements as part of their overall mission. The lands under NPS stewardship provide many excellent locations for monitoring climatic conditions.

It is essential that park units within the SIEN have an effective climate-monitoring system in place to track climate changes and to aid in management decisions relating to these changes. The purpose of this report is to determine the current status of weather and climate monitoring within the SIEN. In this report, we provide the following informational elements:

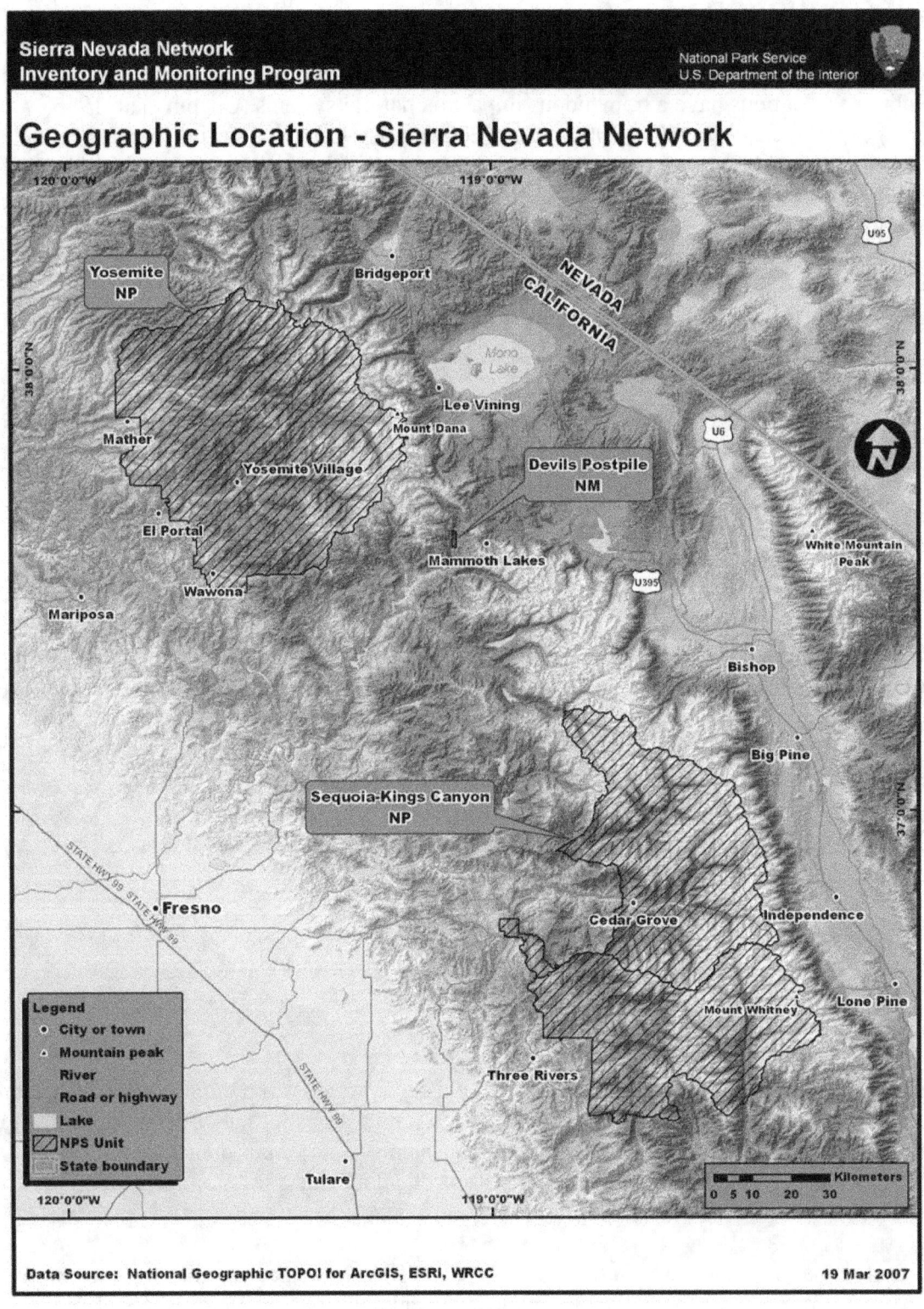

Figure 1.1. Map of the Sierra Nevada Network.

- Overview of broad-scale climatic factors and zones important to SIEN park units.
- Inventory of locations for all weather stations in and near SIEN park units that are relevant (i.e., within a 40 km buffer) to the NPS I&M networks.
- Metadata inventory for each station, including weather-monitoring network affiliations, types of recorded measurements, and information about actual measurements (length of record, etc.).
- Initial evaluation of the adequacy of coverage for existing weather stations and recommendations for improvements in monitoring weather and climate.

The primary objectives of climate- and weather-monitoring activities in SIEN are as follows (Mutch et al. 2005):

A. Determine trends in temperature, precipitation and other meteorological parameters in key locations across the SIEN parks' landscapes.
B. Provide park managers and cooperators with monthly and annual weather summaries as they pertain to other physical and biological monitoring and management programs.
C. Determine changes in precipitation type, timing, intensity, duration, and geographic distribution in SIEN parks.

1.1. Network Terminology

Before proceeding, it is important to stress that this report discusses the idea of "networks" in two different ways. Modifiers are used to distinguish between NPS I&M networks and weather/climate station networks. See Appendix A for a full definition of these terms.

1.1.1. Weather and Climate Station Networks

Most weather and climate measurements are made not from isolated stations but from stations that are part of a network operated in support of a particular mission. The limiting case is a network of one station, where measurements are made by an interested observer or group. Larger networks usually have additional inventory data and station-tracking procedures. Some national weather and climate station networks are associated with the National Oceanic and Atmospheric Administration (NOAA), including the National Weather Service (NWS) Cooperative Observer Program (COOP). Other national networks include the interagency Remote Automated Weather Station (RAWS) network and the U.S. Department of Agriculture/Natural Resources Conservation Service (USDA/NRCS) Snowfall Telemetry (SNOTEL) and snowcourse networks. Usually a single agency, but sometimes a consortium of interested parties, will jointly support a particular weather or climate network.

1.1.2. NPS I&M Networks

Within the NPS, the system for inventorying and monitoring various attributes in the participating park units (about 270–280 in total) is divided into 32 NPS I&M networks. These networks are collections of park units grouped together around a common theme, typically geographical.

1.2. Weather versus Climate Definitions

It is also important to distinguish whether the primary use of a given station is for weather purposes or for climate purposes. Weather station networks are intended for near-real-time usage, where the precise circumstances of a set of measurements are typically less important. In these cases, changes in exposure or other attributes over time are not as critical. Climate station networks, however, are intended for long-term tracking of atmospheric conditions. Siting and exposure are critical factors for climate networks, and it is vitally important that the observational circumstances remain essentially unchanged over the duration of the station record.

Some climate networks can be considered hybrids of weather and climate networks. These hybrid climate networks can supply information on a short-term "weather" time scale and a longer-term "climate" time scale. In this report, "weather" generally refers to current (or near-real-time) atmospheric conditions, while "climate" is defined as the complete ensemble of statistical descriptors for temporal and spatial properties of atmospheric behavior (see Appendix A). Climate and weather phenomena shade gradually into each other and are ultimately inseparable.

1.3. Purpose of Measurements

Climate inventory and monitoring climate activities should be based on a set of guiding fundamental principles. Any evaluation of weather and climate monitoring programs begins with asking the following question:

- What is the purpose of weather and climate measurements?

Evaluation of past, present, or planned weather and climate monitoring activities must be based on the answer to this question.

Weather and climate data and information constitute a prominent and widely requested component of the NPS I&M networks (I&M 2006). Within the context of the NPS, the following services constitute the main purposes for recording weather and climate observations:

- Provide measurements for real-time operational needs and early warnings of potential hazards (landslides, mudflows, washouts, fallen trees, plowing activities, fire conditions, aircraft and watercraft conditions, road conditions, rescue conditions, fog, restoration and remediation activities, etc.).
- Provide visitor education and aid interpretation of expected and actual conditions for visitors while they are in the park and for deciding if and when to visit the park.
- Establish engineering and design criteria for structures, roads, culverts, etc., for human comfort, safety, and economic needs.
- Consistently monitor climate over the long-term to detect changes in environmental drivers affecting ecosystems, including both gradual and sudden events.
- Provide retrospective data to understand *a posteriori* changes in flora and fauna.
- Document for posterity the physical conditions in and near the park units, including mean, extreme, and variable measurements (in time and space) for all applications.

The last three items in the preceding list are pertinent primarily to the NPS I&M networks; however, all items are important to NPS operations and management. Most of the needs in this list overlap heavily. It is often impractical to operate separate climate measuring systems that also cannot be used to meet ordinary weather needs, where there is greater emphasis on timeliness and reliability.

1.4. Design of Climate-Monitoring Programs

Determining the purposes for collecting measurements in a given weather and climate monitoring program will guide the process of identifying weather and climate stations suitable for the monitoring program. The context for making these decisions is provided in Chapter 2 where background on the SIEN climate is presented. However, this process is only one step in evaluating and designing a monitoring program. The following steps must also be included:

- Define park and network-specific monitoring needs and objectives.
- Identify locations and data repositories of existing and historic stations.
- Acquire existing data when necessary or practical.
- Evaluate the quality of existing data.
- Evaluate the adequacy of coverage of existing stations.
- Develop a protocol for monitoring the weather and climate, including the following:
  o Standardized summaries and reports of weather/climate data.
  o Data management (quality assurance and quality control, archiving, data access, etc.).
- Develop and implement a plan for installing or modifying stations, as necessary.

Throughout the design process, there are various factors that require consideration in evaluating weather and climate measurements. Many of these factors have been summarized by the NOAA National Climatic Data Center (NCDC), and widely distributed as the "Ten Principles for Climate Monitoring" (Karl et al. 1996; NRC 2001). These principles are presented in Appendix B, and the guidelines are embodied in many of the comments made throughout this report. The most critical factors are presented here. In addition, an overview of requirements necessary to operate a climate network is provided in Appendix C, with further discussion in Appendix D.

1.4.1. Need for Consistency

A principal goal in climate monitoring is to detect and characterize slow and sudden changes in climate through time. This is of less concern for day-to-day weather changes, but it is of paramount importance for climate variability and change. There are many ways whereby changes in techniques for making measurements, changes in instruments or their exposures, or seemingly innocuous changes in site characteristics can lead to apparent changes in climate. Safeguards must be in place to avoid these false sources of temporal "climate" variability if we are to draw correct inferences about climate behavior over time from archived measurements.

For climate monitoring, consistency through time is vital, counting at least as important as absolute accuracy. Sensors record only what is occurring at the sensor—this is all they can detect. It is the responsibility of station or station network managers to ensure that observations are representative of the spatial and temporal climate scales that we wish to record.

1.4.2. Metadata

Changes in instruments, site characteristics, and observing methodologies can lead to apparent changes in climate through time. It is therefore vital to document all factors that can bear on the interpretation of climate measurements and to update the information repeatedly through time.

This information ("metadata," data about data) has its own history and set of quality-control issues that parallel those of the actual data. There is no single standard for the content of climate metadata, but a simple rule suffices:

- Observers should record all information that could be needed in the future to interpret observations correctly without benefit of the observers' personal recollections.

Such documentation includes notes, drawings, site forms, and photos, which can be of inestimable value if taken in the correct manner. That stated, it is not always clear to the metadata provider *what is important* for posterity and *what will be important* in the future. It is almost impossible to "over document" a station. Station documentation is greatly underappreciated and is seldom thorough enough (especially for climate purposes). Insufficient attention to this issue often lowers the present and especially future value of otherwise useful data.

The convention followed throughout climatology is to refer to metadata as information about the measurement process, station circumstances, and data. The term "data" is reserved solely for the actual weather and climate records obtained from sensors.

1.4.3. Maintenance

Inattention to maintenance is the greatest source of failure in weather and climate station networks. Problems begin to occur soon after sites are deployed. A regular visit schedule must be implemented, where sites, settings (e.g., vegetation), sensors, communications, and data flow are checked routinely (once or twice a year at a minimum) and updated as necessary. Parts must be changed out for periodic recalibration or replacement. With adequate maintenance, the entire instrument suite should be replaced or completely refurbished about once every five to seven years.

Simple preventive maintenance is effective but requires much planning and skilled technical staff. Changes in technology and products require retraining and continual re-education. Travel, logistics, scheduling, and seasonal access restrictions consume major amounts of time and budget but are absolutely necessary. Without such attention, data gradually become less credible and then often are misused or not used at all.

1.4.4. Automated versus Manual Stations

Historic stations often have depended on manual observations and many continue to operate in this mode. Manual observations frequently produce excellent data sets. Sensors and data are simple and intuitive, well tested, and relatively cheap. Manual stations have much to offer in certain circumstances and can be a source of both primary and backup data. However, methodical consistency for manual measurements is a constant challenge, especially with a mobile work force. Operating manual stations takes time and needs to be done on a regular schedule, though sometimes the routine is welcome.

Nearly all newer stations are automated. Automated stations provide better time resolution, increased (though imperfect) reliability, greater capacity for data storage, and improved accessibility to large amounts of data. The purchase cost for automated stations is higher than for manual stations. A common expectation and serious misconception is that an automated station can be deployed and left to operate on its own. In reality, automation does not eliminate the need for people but rather changes the type of person that is needed. Skilled technical personnel are needed and must be readily available, especially if live communications exist and data gaps are not wanted. Site visits are needed at least annually and spare parts must be maintained. Typical annual costs for sensors and maintenance are $1500–2500 per station per year but these costs still can vary greatly depending on the kind of automated site.

1.4.5. Communications
With manual stations, the observer is responsible for recording and transmitting station data. Data from automated stations, however, can be transmitted quickly for access by research and operations personnel, which is a highly preferable situation. A comparison of communication systems for automated and manual stations shows that automated stations generally require additional equipment, more power, higher transmission costs, attention to sources of disruption or garbling, and backup procedures (e.g., manual downloads from data loggers).

Automated stations are capable of functioning normally without communication and retaining many months of data. At such sites, however, alerts about station problems are not possible, large gaps can accrue when accessible stations quit, and the constituencies needed to support such stations are smaller and less vocal. Two-way communications permit full recovery from disruptions, ability to reprogram data loggers remotely, and better opportunities for diagnostics and troubleshooting. In virtually all cases, two-way communications are much preferred to all other communication methods. However, two-way communications require considerations of cost, signal access, transmission rates, interference, and methods for keeping sensor and communication power loops separate. Two-way communications are frequently impossible (no service) or impractical, expensive, or power consumptive. Two-way methods (cellular, land line, radio, Internet) require smaller up-front costs as compared to other methods of communication and have variable recurrent costs, starting at zero. Satellite links work everywhere (except when blocked by trees or cliffs) and are quite reliable but are one-way and relatively slow, allow no re-transmissions, and require high up-front costs ($3000–4000) but no recurrent costs. Communications technology is changing constantly and requires vigilant attention by maintenance personnel.

1.4.6. Quality Assurance and Quality Control
Quality control and quality assurance are issues at every step through the entire sequence of sensing, communication, storage, retrieval, and display of environmental data. Quality assurance is an umbrella concept that covers all data collection and processing (start-to-finish) and ensures that credible information is available to the end user. Quality control has a more limited scope and is defined by the International Standards Organization as "the operational techniques and activities that are used to satisfy quality requirements." The central problem can be better appreciated if we approach quality control in the following way.

- Quality control is the evaluation, assessment, and rehabilitation of imperfect data by utilizing other imperfect data.

7

The quality of the data only decreases with time once the observation is made. The best and most effective quality control, therefore, consists in making high-quality measurements from the start and then successfully transmitting the measurements to an ingest process and storage site. Once the data are received from a monitoring station, a series of checks with increasing complexity can be applied, ranging from single-element checks (self-consistency) to multiple-element checks (inter-sensor consistency) to multiple-station/single-element checks (inter-station consistency). Suitable ancillary data (battery voltages, data ranges for all measurements, etc.) can prove extremely useful in diagnosing problems.

There is rarely a single technique in quality control procedures that will work satisfactorily for all situations. Quality-control procedures must be tailored to individual station circumstances, data access and storage methods, and climate regimes.

The fundamental issue in quality control centers on the tradeoff between falsely rejecting good data (Type I error) and falsely accepting bad data (Type II error). We cannot reduce the incidence of one type of error without increasing the incidence of the other type. In weather and climate data assessments, since good data are absolutely crucial for interpreting climate records properly, Type I errors are deemed far less desirable than Type II errors.

Not all observations are equal in importance. Quality-control procedures are likely to have the greatest difficulty evaluating the most extreme observations, where independent information usually must be sought and incorporated. Quality-control procedures involving more than one station usually involve a great deal of infrastructure with its own (imperfect) error-detection methods, which must be in place before a single value can be evaluated.

1.4.7. Standards

Although there is near-universal recognition of the value in systematic weather and climate measurements, these measurements will have little value unless they conform to accepted standards. There is not a single source for standards for collecting weather and climate data nor a single standard that meets all needs. Measurement standards have been developed by the World Meteorological Organization (WMO 1983; 2005), the American Association of State Climatologists (AASC 1985), the U.S. Environmental Protection Agency (EPA 1987), Finklin and Fischer (1990), the RAWS program (Bureau of Land Management [BLM] 1997), and the National Wildfire Coordinating Group (2004). Variations to these measurement standards also have been offered by instrument makers (e.g., Tanner 1990).

1.4.8. Who Makes the Measurements?

The lands under NPS stewardship provide many excellent locations to host the monitoring of climate by the NPS or other collaborators. These lands are largely protected from human development and other land changes that can impact observed climate records. Most park units historically have observed weather/climate elements as part of their overall mission. Many of these measurements come from station networks managed by other agencies, with observations taken or overseen by NPS personnel, in some cases, or by collaborators from the other agencies. Park units that are small, lack sufficient resources, or lack sites presenting adequate exposure may benefit by utilizing weather/climate measurements collected from nearby stations.

2.0. Climate Background

Climatic forces are a major driver of Sierra Nevada ecosystems. Current patterns of vegetation, water dynamics, and animal distribution in the Sierra Nevada are determined largely by cumulative effects of past and present climates. (Mutch et al. 2005). It is essential that the SIEN park units have an effective climate monitoring system to track climate changes and to aid in management decisions relating to these changes. In order to do this, it is essential to understand the climate characteristics of the SIEN, as discussed in this chapter.

2.1. Climate and the SIEN Environment

Topographical influences are instrumental in defining the climate of the SIEN (Mutch et al. 2005). Strong climatic gradients develop with changing elevation in the Sierra Nevada, from west to east. Low to mid-elevations have a Mediterranean-type climate, which is characterized by hot, dry summers and cool, wet winters. Higher elevations are dominated by a Microthermal (or Boreal) climate, which is characterized by having average temperatures of the coldest month below -3°C. As a result, steep temperature gradients occur in SIEN park units, with the severity of these gradients dependent on factors such as slope aspect and vegetation cover (Stephenson 1988). The wettest conditions occur on the western slopes of the Sierra Nevada. Above 2000 m, much of the precipitation falls as snow (Stephenson 1988), creating a significant snowpack in the montane and subalpine elevations. Over the highest alpine zones, much of the moisture has been lost from the clouds and the amount of snow accumulating on the ground begins to decline with increasing elevation. East of the crest, the mountains create a rain shadow with significantly less precipitation falling throughout the season. Precipitation also increases with latitude, due to increasingly close proximity to the main winter storm track as one heads north across the SIEN.

Average global temperatures have been rising, with the earth's atmosphere currently being warmer than at any point during the last several centuries (Mann et al. 1998). Much of this globally-averaged increase in temperature may possibly be due to anthropogenic influences (Houghton et al. 2001). The last several decades in the Sierra Nevada were among the warmest of the last millennium (Graumlich 1993). Phenological studies indicated that in much of the West, lilacs and honeysuckles are responding to the warming trend by blooming and leafing out earlier (Cayan et al. 2001). Observed warming trends in temperature are significantly associated with discernible changes in plant and animal phenological traits (Root et al. 2005). Spring snowmelt flows in many western streams are beginning earlier than they did in the mid-twentieth century (Cayan et al. 2001; Dettinger 2005a; Lundquist et al. 2005). There is also a trend towards slightly later precipitation (Dettinger 2005a, b). Observed streamflow timing and winter-spring warming trends are consistent with current projections of how greenhouse effects may influence western climates and hydrology.

Paleoecological records hint at what future climate conditions in the SIEN could be like in response to ongoing and projected climate changes. The early and middle Holocene (ca. 10000 to 4500 years ago) was a period of generally higher global summer temperatures and prolonged summer drought in the SIEN. During this period, fire regimes and vegetation community composition of Sierra Nevada forests differed from those of today, with forests being much more dominated by pines (Anderson 1990; Anderson and Smith 1991; Anderson 1994; Anderson and Smith 1994; 1997).

Further projected increases in global temperatures are expected to have profound effects on SIEN weather and climate, which in turn will have a large impact on SIEN ecosystems (Mutch et al. 2005). Recent simulations of climate change models suggest that by the years 2050 to 2100, average annual temperature in the Sierra Nevada could increase by as much as 3.8°C (Snyder et al. 2002)—the equivalent of an upward displacement in climatic zones of several hundred meters. Global warming is likely to shift habitats to higher elevations. Some organisms with limited mobility or specific habitat needs (e.g., amphibians) may not be able to move or survive such habitat shifts and could be locally extirpated. Consequently, species diversity may decline. Some habitats (e.g., high alpine) may shrink dramatically or disappear entirely, leading to irreversible loss of some species (e.g., Clark's Nutcracker). Increasing drought stress could increase mortality among adult trees (Dettinger 2005b), as they would be more vulnerable to insects, pathogens, and air pollution. Some model predictions indicate a reduction in alpine and subalpine forests in the Sierra (Hayhoe et al. 2004). A warmer climate would allow certain species—e.g., those species unable to get a stronghold because of cold temperatures—to thrive and reproduce. Some models predict future climate change will be accompanied by increased lightning strikes at latitudes spanned by the Sierra Nevada (Price and Rind 1991). Compounding the increase in wildfire ignitions, extreme weather conditions such as drought are likely to result in fires burning larger areas, being more severe, and escaping containment more frequently (Torn and Fried 1992; Miller and Urban 1999). There are numerous ecological consequences including, but not limited to, degraded water quality, vegetation type conversions, and changes in habitat and species types.

It is predicted that even a relatively modest mean temperature increase (2.5°C) would significantly alter hydrologic processes including precipitation patterns, snowpack, and surface water dynamics (e.g., flow). The most pronounced changes would probably be earlier snowmelt runoff, reduced summer base flows and soil moisture (Dettinger et al. 2004; Stewart et al. 2004,2005; Dettinger 2005a), a lower snowpack volume at mid-elevations (Knowles and Cayan 2002), and increased winter and spring flooding (Dettinger et al. 2004). Changes in precipitation type and timing could result (Knowles et al. 2006), which may result in longer and drier summers, i.e., less water available during the months it is most needed (Dettinger 2005a). Glacial extent in the Sierra Nevada has declined markedly in the past several decades (Mutch et al. 2005). Recent studies on snowpack trends in the Sierra Nevada since the middle of the twentieth century present mixed results (Dozier 2004; Hamlet et al. 2005; Howat and Tulaczyk 2005; Mote et al. 2005; Knowles et al. 2006), either showing no changes or decreases in snowpack. If Sierra Nevada snowpack decreases in the future as some climate model predictions indicate (NAST 2001), the "natural reservoirs" provided by snowpack will become progressively less useful for water resources management, flood risk may change in unpredictable ways, and Sierra Nevada ecosystems will experience increasingly severe summer-drought conditions (Dettinger 2005a; Dettinger et al. 2005; Mote et al. 2005).

2.2. Spatial Variability

Precipitation characteristics of the SIEN are defined by the superimposed effects of topography and the orientation of major ranges with respect to the prevailing storm tracks (from the west). Precipitation generally increases towards the west, with the highest precipitation totals occurring at higher elevations on south- and west-facing slopes. This pattern is evident particularly in SEKI, where the western mountains receive up to 1200 mm of precipitation each year, while the

Sierra Crest itself, in eastern SEKI, only receives up to 1000 mm each year. The wettest locations within the SIEN occur in northernmost portions of YOSE that are west of the Sierra Crest. In these locations, mean annual precipitation totals generally exceed 1400 mm (Figure 2.1). Lower elevations within YOSE, such as Yosemite Village, receive less than 1000 mm of precipitation each year. The driest locations within the SIEN occur at SEKI, where the southeastern portions of the park unit can receive less than 600 mm on average each year, partially due to rainshadowing effects from the Great Western Divide in south-central SEKI. Although it is not the driest location in the SIEN, DEPO is still relatively dry due to its lower elevation and some rainshadowing effects from the mountains to the west. This park unit typically receives between 600 and 800 mm of precipitation each year. Much of the precipitation in SIEN park units occurs during the winter months (Figure 2.2). Across elevations and latitudes, nearly 70% of precipitation falls from December through March and only about 4% from June through September (Stephenson 1988). As a result, much SIEN precipitation occurs as snow, particularly for the higher elevations in the SIEN park units, where over 10 m of snowfall occur regularly (Figure 2.3). The highest snowfall totals occur in the highest elevations of SEKI. To the north, in YOSE, more frequent storms occur but these storms tend to have less heavy snowfall with them compared to storms that impact SEKI. Also, being a few hundred meters lower in elevation than SEKI, the higher elevations of YOSE also tend to see more rain as well as snow during the winter months, thus decreasing snowfall totals.

Mean annual temperatures across the SIEN are driven largely by elevation. The warmest temperatures occur in the lower elevations that occur in western portions of both SEKI and YOSE (Figure 2.4). In YOSE, an east-west temperature gradient is very evident, with the highest elevations in the eastern side of the park unit seeing mean annual temperatures around 0°C. The westernmost portions of YOSE, including Yosemite Valley, see mean annual temperatures that are greater than 9°C. Mean annual temperatures in DEPO are just over 3°C. The warmest annually-averaged temperatures occur in southwestern SEKI, in the Kaweah River watershed. Areas just northeast of Three Rivers see mean annual temperatures that exceed 15°C. The coolest conditions in the SIEN also occur in SEKI, at the highest elevations of the park unit. Mean annual temperatures in these areas do not exceed -3°C.

Topographical influences are also quite significant for both winter and summer temperatures in the SIEN. The coldest winter temperatures in the SIEN occur at the highest elevations of SEKI, where January minimum temperatures generally get below -18°C (Figure 2.5). In contrast, the lowest elevations in the western portions of both SEKI and YOSE see January minimum temperatures that are just below freezing (0°C). The warmest minimum temperatures occur in southwestern SEKI, staying just above freezing on average. Winter minimum temperatures in DEPO are generally near -10°C. Temperatures can become quite warm or even hot at lower elevations of SIEN park units during the summer months. July maximum temperatures in the valleys of western YOSE, including Yosemite Valley, approach 30°C. The warmest locations, in southwestern portions of SEKI, usually exceed 33°C (Figure 2.6). Higher elevations experience much cooler conditions. Mean maximum temperatures in July at the higher elevations of YOSE are below 18°C. The highest elevations of SEKI are even cooler than this, with July maximum temperatures staying well below 12°C.

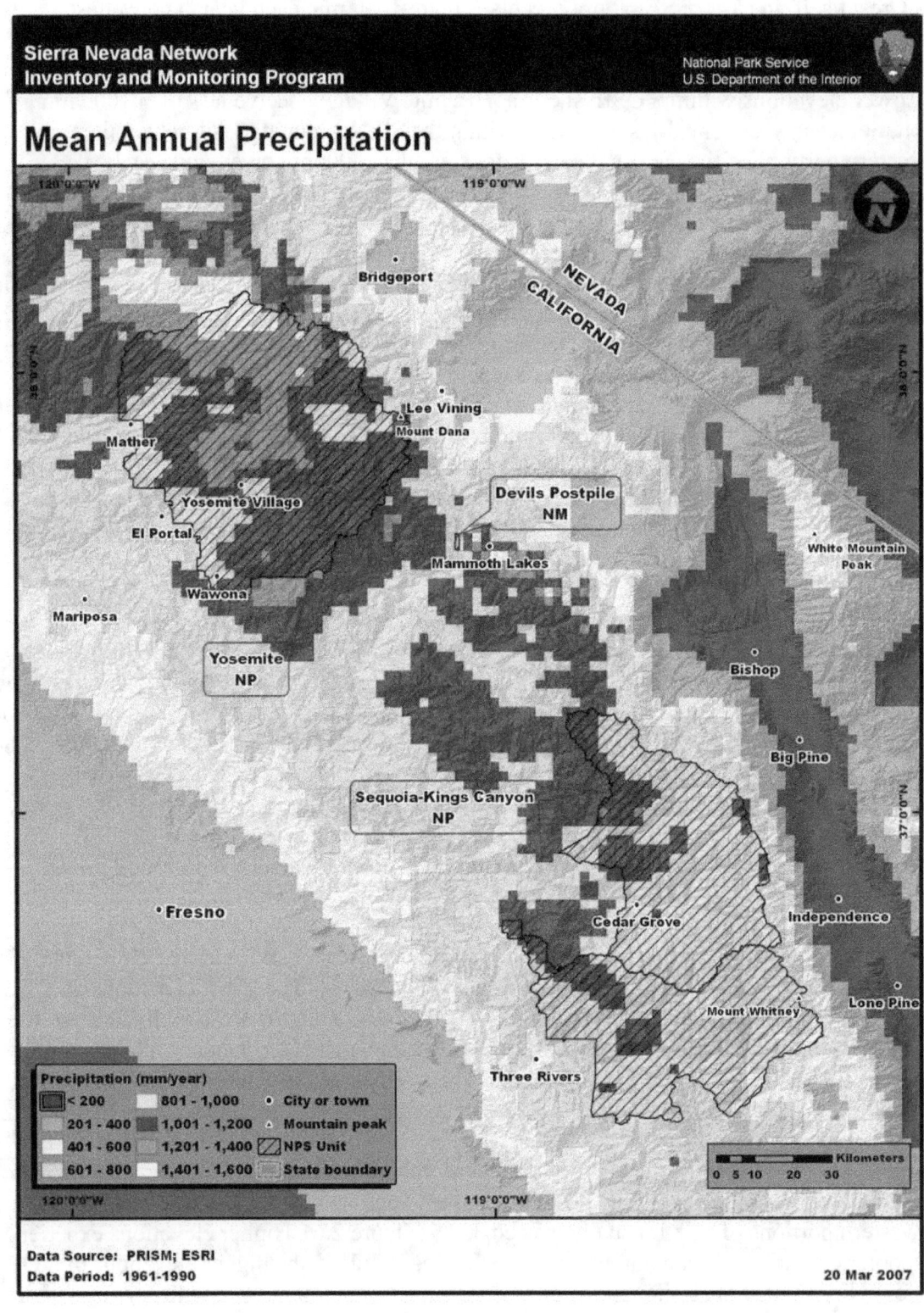

Figure 2.1. Mean annual precipitation, 1961-1990, for the SIEN.

a)

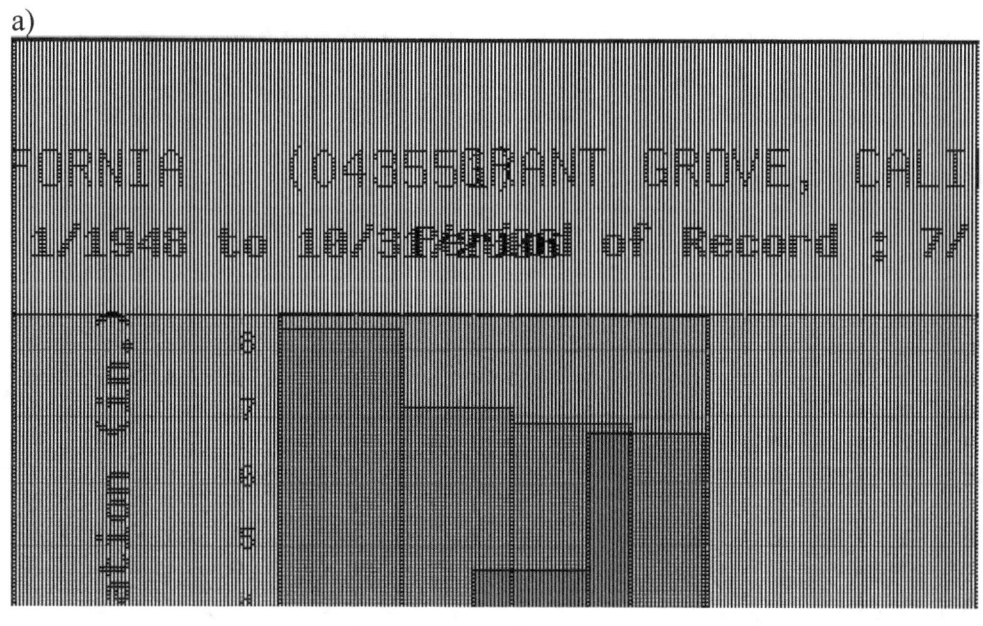

b)

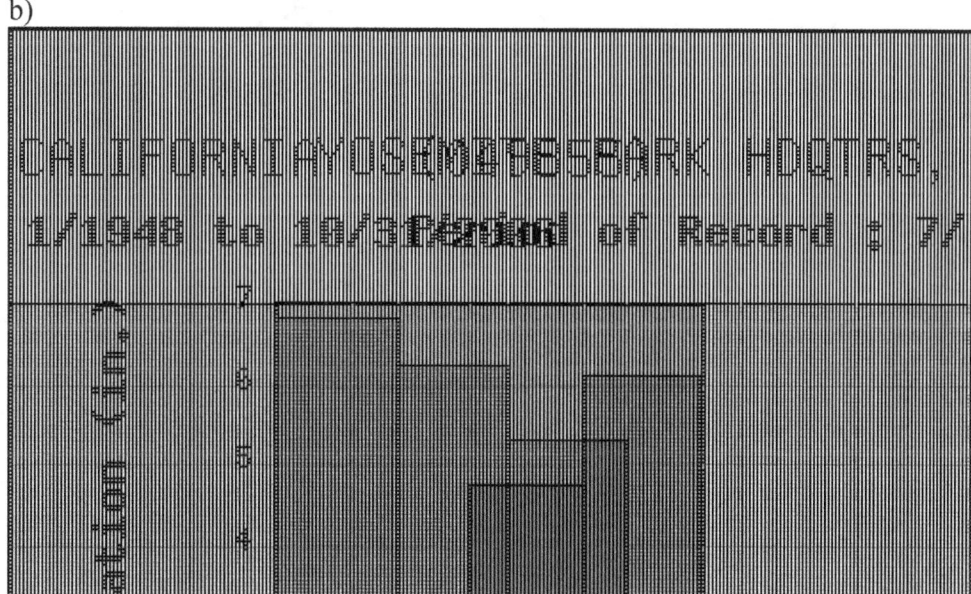

Figure 2.2. Mean monthly precipitation at selected locations in the SIEN, including SEKI (a) and YOSE (b).

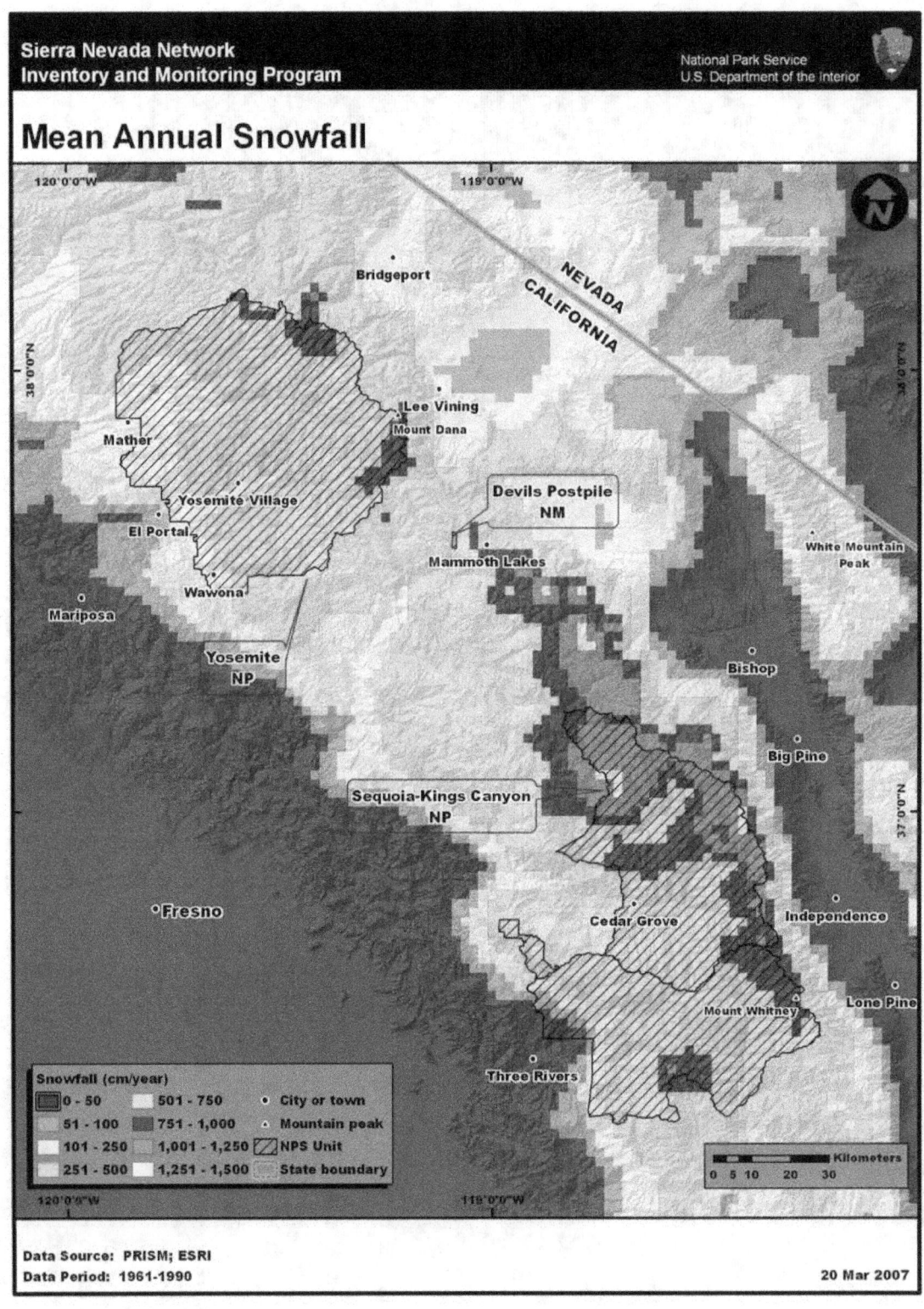

Figure 2.3. Mean annual snowfall, 1961-1990, for the SIEN. Snowfall values are from PRISM (Parameter Regression on Independent Slopes Model), derived from PRISM monthly temperature and precipitation fields.

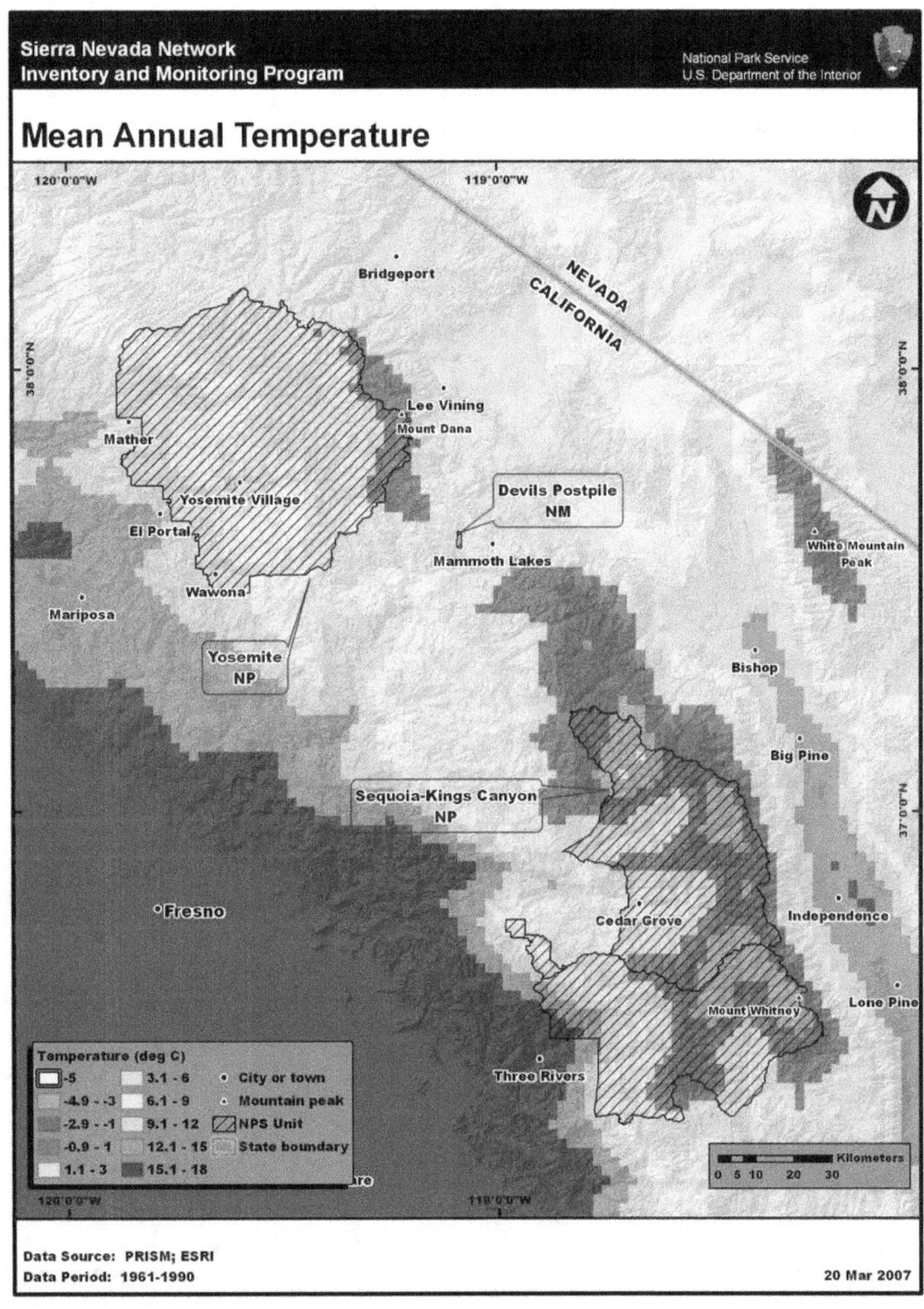

Figure 2.4. Mean annual temperature, 1961-1990, for the SIEN.

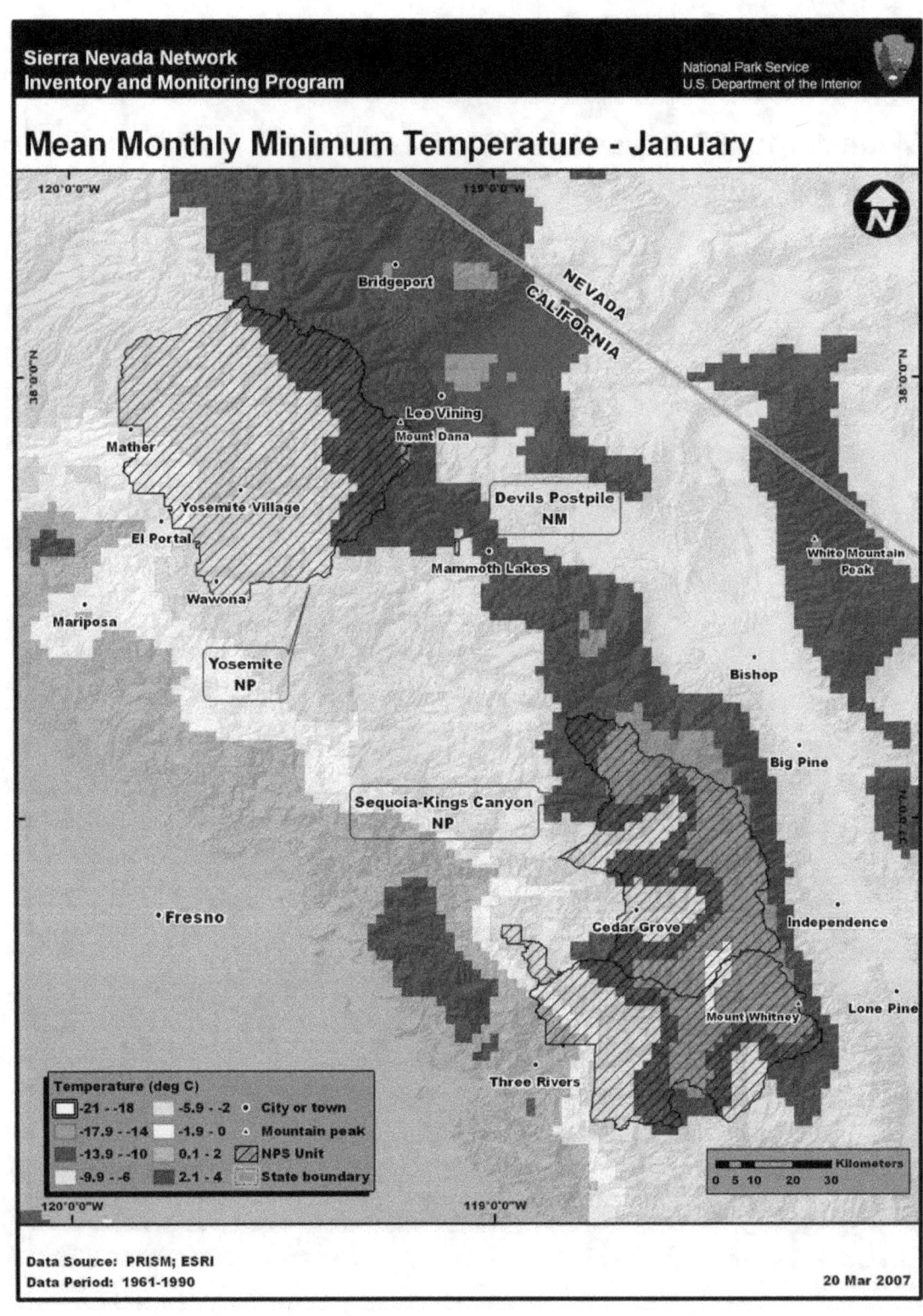

Figure 2.5. Mean January minimum temperature, 1961-1990, for the SIEN.

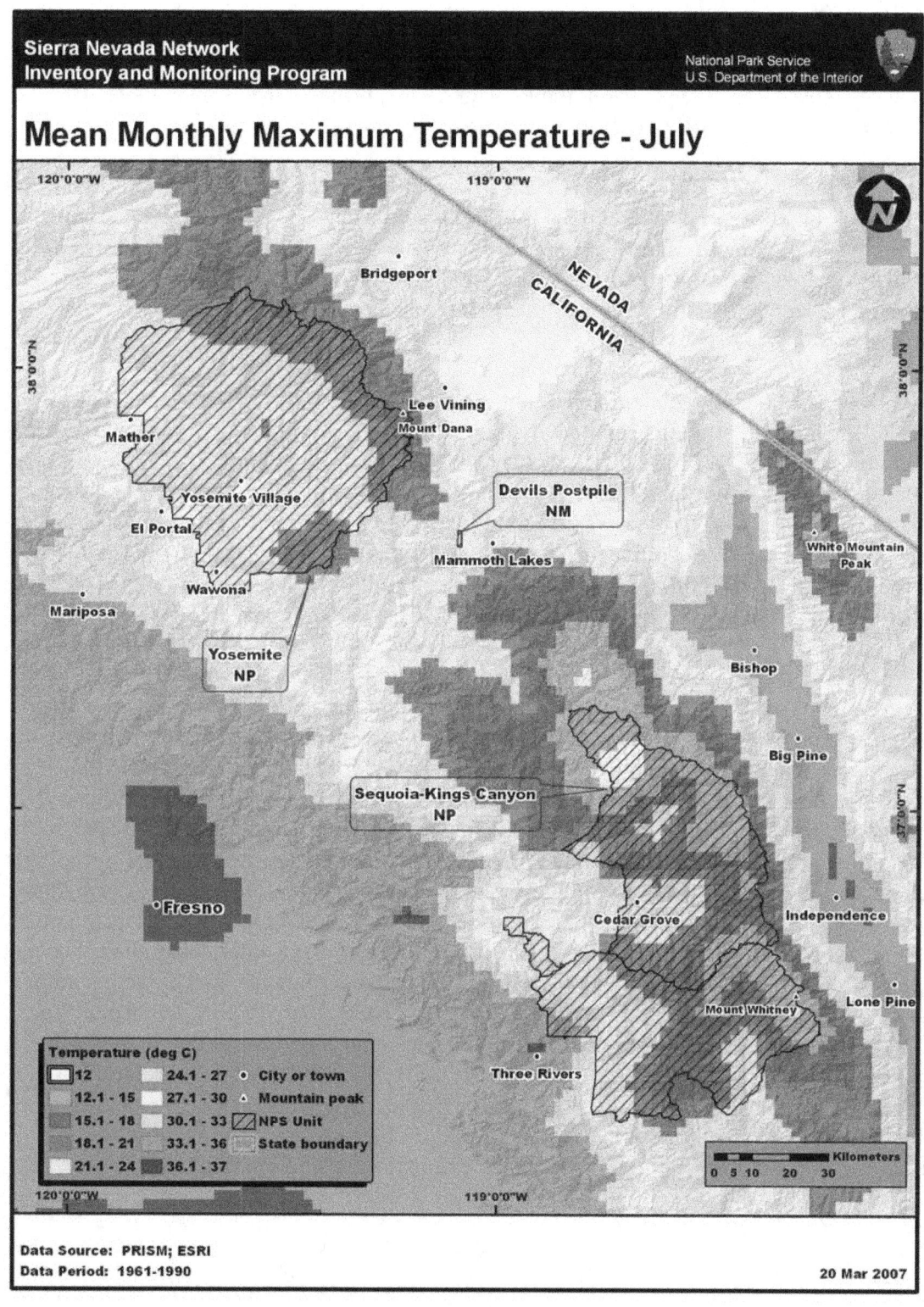

Figure 2.6. Mean July maximum temperature, 1961-1990, for the SIEN.

2.3. Temporal Variability

The Pacific-North America Oscillation (PNA; Wallace and Gutzler 1981) is an important contributor to variability of storm frequencies and tracks during a given year, with variations on the order of weeks. Negative phases of the PNA generally bring cooler temperatures and increased storminess over the SIEN.

Both the El Niño Southern Oscillation (ENSO) and the Pacific Decadal Oscillation (PDO) cause interannual climate variations in the SIEN (Redmond and Koch 1991; Mock 1996; Cayan et al. 1998; Mantua 2000; Mantua and Hare 2002). El Niño conditions and/or positive phases of the PDO are associated with cooler and wetter conditions, particularly in southern SIEN, while La Niña conditions and/or negative phases of the PDO are associated with warmer and drier conditions.

An investigation of daily precipitation amounts around the SIEN region over the last century (Figure 2.7) reveals little in the way of an overall trend. However, long-term trends in ambient temperature for the SIEN (Figure 2.8) indicate that temperatures have become significantly warmer over the past several decades. This finding is in line with other studies of temperature trends over the western U.S. (NAST 2001). However, it is not clear how much of this observed pattern may be due to discontinuities in temperature records at individual stations, caused by artificial changes such as station moves. These patterns highlight the emphasis on measurement consistency that is needed in order to properly detect long-term climatic changes.

2.4. Parameter Regression on Independent Slopes Model

The climate maps presented in this report were generated using the Parameter Regression on Independent Slopes Model (PRISM). This model was developed to address the extreme spatial and elevation gradients exhibited by the climate of the western United States (Daly et al. 1994; 2002; Gibson et al. 2002; Doggett et al. 2004). The maps produced through PRISM have undergone rigorous evaluation in the western U.S. This model originally was developed to provide climate information at scales matching available land-cover maps to assist in ecologic modeling. The PRISM technique accounts for the scale-dependent effects of topography on mean values of climate elements. Elevation provides the first-order constraint for the mapped climate fields, with slope and orientation (aspect) providing second-order constraints. The model has been enhanced gradually to address inversions, coast/land gradients, and climate patterns in small-scale trapping basins. Monthly climate fields are generated by PRISM to account for seasonal variations in elevation gradients in climate elements. These monthly climate fields then can be combined into seasonal and annual climate fields. Since PRISM maps are grid maps, they do not replicate point values but rather, for a given grid cell, represent the grid-cell average of the climate variable in question at the average elevation for that cell. The model relies on observed surface and upper-air measurements to estimate spatial climate fields.

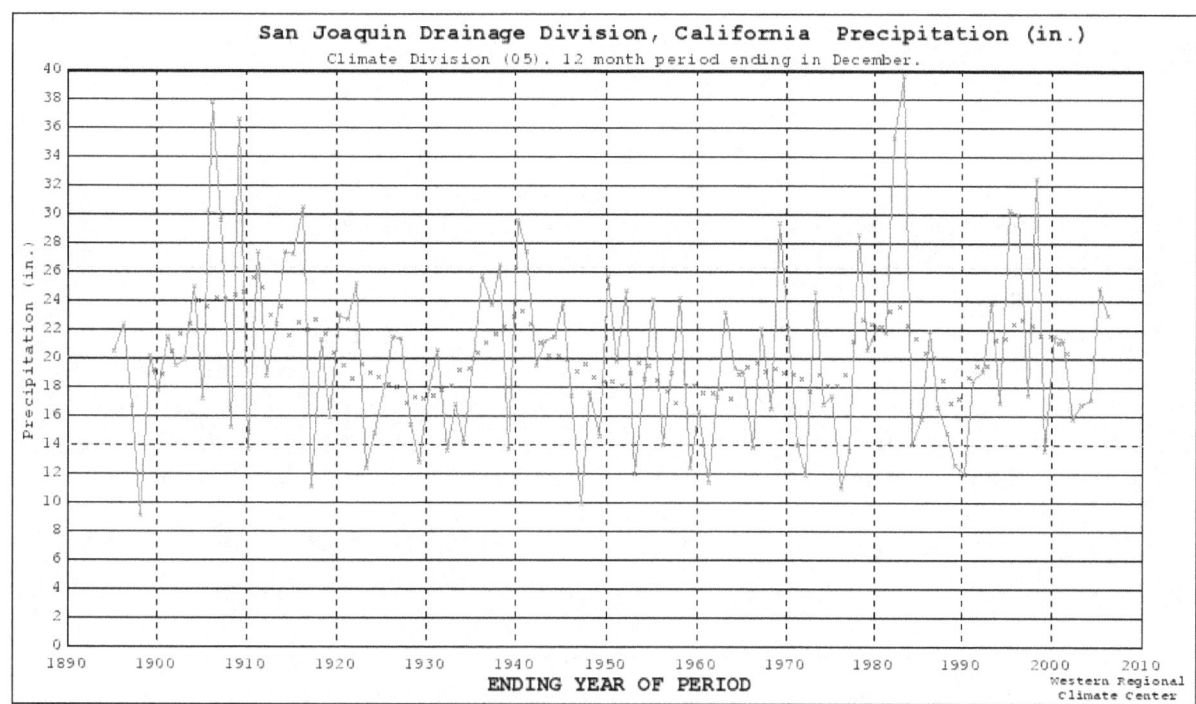

Figure 2.7. Precipitation time series, 1895-2005, for the SIEN. These include twelve-month precipitation (ending in December) (red), 10-year running mean (blue), mean (green), and plus/minus one standard deviation (green dotted).

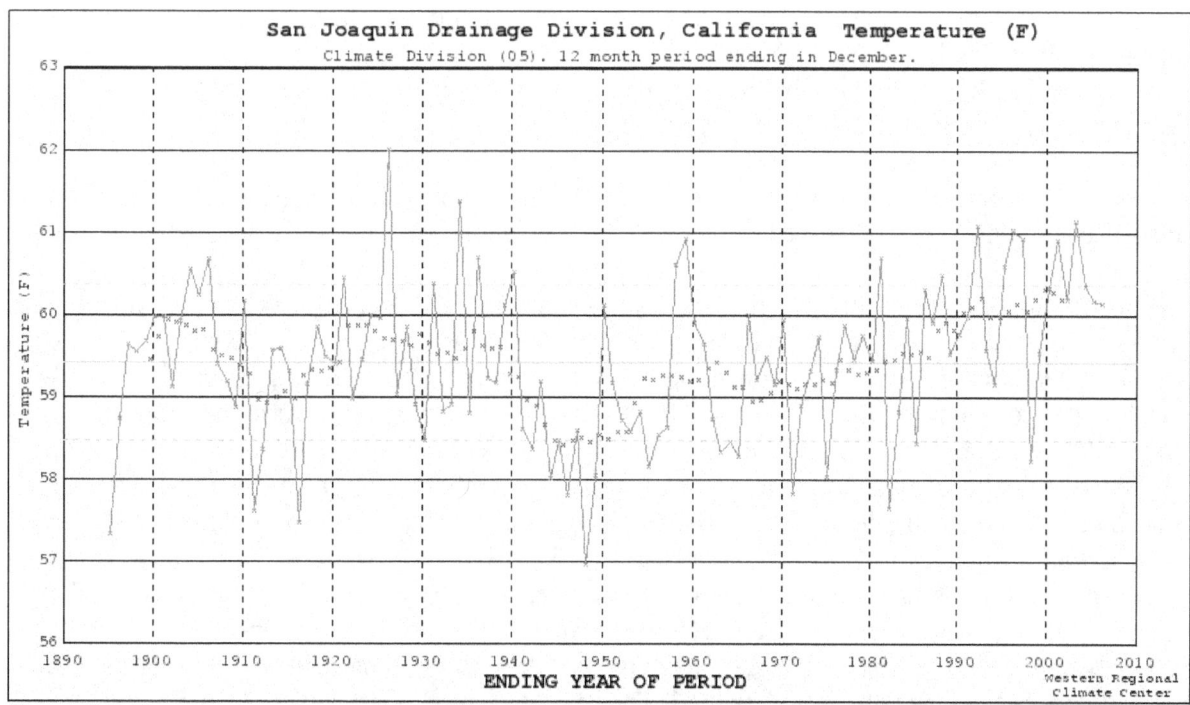

Figure 2.8. Temperature time series, 1895-2005, for the SIEN. These include twelve-month average temperature (ending in December) (red), 10-year running mean (blue), mean (green), and plus/minus one standard deviation (green dotted).

19

3.0. Methods

Having discussed the climatic characteristics of the SIEN, we now present the procedures that were used to obtain information for weather and climate stations within the SIEN. This information was obtained from various sources, as mentioned in the following paragraphs. Retrieval of station metadata constituted a major component of this work.

3.1. Metadata Retrieval

A key component of station inventories is determining the kinds of observations that have been conducted over time, by whom, and in what manner; when each type of observation began and ended; and whether these observations are still being conducted. Metadata about the observational process (Table 3.1) generally consist of a series of vignettes that apply to time intervals and, therefore, constitute a *history* rather than a single snapshot. An expanded list of relevant metadata fields for this inventory is provided in Appendix E. This report has relied on metadata records from three sources: (a) Western Regional Climate Center (WRCC), (b) NPS personnel, and (c) other knowledgeable personnel, such as state climate office staff.

The initial metadata sources for this report were stored at WRCC. This regional climate center (RCC) acts as a working repository of many western climate records, including the main networks outlined in this section. The WRCC conducts live and periodic data collection (ingests) from all major national and western weather and climate networks. These networks include the COOP network, the Surface Airways Observation network (SAO) operated by NWS and the Federal Aviation Administration (FAA), the interagency RAWS network, and various smaller networks. The WRCC is expanding its capability to ingest information from other networks as resources permit and usefulness dictates. This center has relied heavily on historic archives (in many cases supplemented with live ingests) to assess the quantity (not necessarily quality) of data available for NPS I&M network applications.

The primary source of metadata at WRCC is the Applied Climate Information System (ACIS), a joint effort among RCCs and other NOAA entities. Metadata for SIEN weather/climate stations identified from the ACIS database are available in file "SIEN_from_ACIS.tar.gz" (see Appendix F). Historic metadata pertaining to major climate- and weather-observing systems in the U.S. are stored in ACIS where metadata are linked to the observed data. A distributed system, ACIS is synchronized among the RCCs. Mainstream software is utilized, including Postgress, Python™, and Java™ programming languages; CORBA®-compliant network software; and industry-standard, nonproprietary hardware and software. Metadata and data for all major national climate and weather networks have been entered into the ACIS database. For this project, the available metadata from many smaller networks also have been entered but in most cases the actual data have not yet been entered. Data sets are in the NetCDF (Network Common Data Form) format, but the design allows for integration with legacy systems, including non-NetCDF files (used at WRCC) and additional metadata (added for this project). The ACIS also supports a suite of products to visualize or summarize data from these data sets. National climate-monitoring maps are updated daily using the ACIS data feed. The developmental phases of ACIS have utilized metadata supplied by the NCDC and NWS with many tens of thousands of entries, screened as well as possible for duplications, mistakes, and omissions.

Table 3.1. Primary metadata fields for SIEN weather and climate stations. Explanations are provided as appropriate.

Metadata Field	Notes
Station name	Station name associated with network listed in "Climate Network."
Latitude	Numerical value (units: see coordinate units).
Longitude	Numerical value (units: see coordinate units).
Coordinate units	Latitude/longitude (units: decimal degrees, degree-minute-second, etc.).
Datum	Datum used as basis for coordinates: WGS 84, NAD 83, etc.
Elevation	Elevation of station above mean sea level (m).
Slope	Slope of ground surface below station (degrees).
Aspect	Azimuth that ground surface below station faces.
Climate division	NOAA climate division where station is located. Climate divisions are NOAA-specified zones sharing similar climate and hydrology characteristics.
Country	Country where station is located.
State	State where station is located.
County	County where station is located.
Weather/climate network	Primary weather/climate network the station belongs to (COOP, RAWS, etc.).
NPS unit code	Four-letter code identifying park unit where station resides.
NPS unit name	Full name of park unit.
NPS unit type	National park, national monument, etc.
UTM zone	If UTM is the only coordinate system available.
Location notes	Useful information not already included in "station narrative."
Climate variables	Temperature, precipitation, etc.
Installation date	Date of station installation.
Removal date	Date of station removal.
Station photograph	Digital image of station.
Photograph date	Date photograph was taken.
Photographer	Name of person who took the photograph.
Station narrative	Anything related to general site description; may include site exposure, characteristics of surrounding vegetation, driving directions, etc.
Contact name	Name of the person involved with station operation.
Organization	Group or agency affiliation of contact person.
Contact type	Designation that identifies contact person as the station owner, observer, maintenance person, data manager, etc.
Position/job title	Official position/job title of contact person.
Address	Address of contact person.
E-mail address	E-mail address of contact person.
Phone	Phone number of contact person (and extension if available).
Contact notes	Other information needed to reach contact person.

In addition to obtaining SIEN weather/climate station metadata from ACIS, metadata were obtained from NPS staff at the SIEN office. The metadata provided from the SIEN office are available in file "SIEN_NPS.tar.gz." Most of the stations noted by SIEN staff are already accounted for in ACIS. We have also relied on information supplied at various times in the past by the BLM, NPS, NCDC, and NWS.

Two types of information have been used to complete the SIEN climate station inventory.

- <u>Station inventories</u>: Information about observational procedures, latitude/longitude, elevation, measured elements, measurement frequency, sensor types, exposures, ground cover and vegetation, data-processing details, network, purpose, and managing individual or agency, etc.

- <u>Data inventories</u>: Information about measured data values including completeness, seasonality, data gaps, representation of missing data, flagging systems, how special circumstances in the data record are denoted, etc.

This is not a straightforward process. Extensive searches are typically required to develop historic station and data inventories. Both types of inventories frequently contain information gaps and often rely on tacit and unrealistic assumptions. Sources of information for these inventories frequently are difficult to recover or are undocumented and unreliable. In many cases, the actual weather and climate data available from different sources are not linked directly to metadata records. To the extent that actual data can be acquired (rather than just metadata), it is possible to cross-check these records and perform additional assessments based on the amount and completeness of the data.

Certain types of weather and climate networks that possess any of the following attributes have not been considered for inclusion in the inventory:

- Private networks with proprietary access and/or inability to obtain or provide sufficient metadata.
- Private weather enthusiasts (often with high-quality data) whose metadata are not available and whose data are not readily accessible.
- Unofficial observers supplying data to the NWS (lack of access to current data and historic archives; lack of metadata).
- Networks having no available historic data.
- Networks having poor-quality metadata.
- Networks having poor access to metadata.
- Real-time networks having poor access to real-time data.

Previous inventory efforts at WRCC have shown that for the networks identified in the preceding list, in light of the need for quality data to track weather and climate, the resources required and difficulty encountered in obtaining metadata or data are prohibitively large.

3.2. Criteria for Locating Stations

To identify weather and climate stations for each park unit in the SIEN we selected only those stations located within 40 km of the SIEN park unit boundaries. This buffer distance was selected in an attempt to include automated stations from major networks such as RAWS and SNOTEL, but also to keep the size of the stations lists to a reasonable number.

The station locator maps presented in Chapter 4 were designed to show clearly the spatial distributions of all major weather/climate station networks in SIEN. We recognize that other mapping formats may be more suitable for other specific needs.

4.0. Station Inventory

An objective of this report is to show the locations of weather and climate stations for the SIEN region in relation to the boundaries of the NPS park units within the SIEN. A station does not have to be within park boundaries to provide useful data and information for a park unit.

4.1. Climate and Weather Networks

Most stations in the SIEN region are associated with at least one of 16 major weather and climate networks (Table 4.1). Brief descriptions of each network are provided below (see Appendix G for greater detail).

Table 4.1. Weather and climate networks represented within the SIEN.

Acronym	Name
BAMI	Bay Area Mesoscale Initiative
CARB	California Air Resources Board
CASTNet	Clean Air Status and Trends Network
CIMIS	California Irrigation Management Information System
COOP	NWS Cooperative Observer Program
CWOP	Citizen Weather Observer Program
DRI	Desert Research Institute network
GPMP	NPS Gaseous Pollutant Monitoring Program
NADP	National Atmospheric Deposition Program
NRCS-SC	NRCS snowcourse network
POMS	Portable Ozone Monitoring System
RAWS	Remote Automated Weather Station network
SAO	NWS/FAA Surface Airways Observation network
SNOTEL	NRCS Snowfall Telemetry network
UCSB	University of California Santa Barbara network
WX4U	Weather For You network

4.1.1. Bay Area Mesoscale Initiative (BAMI)

The BAMI network is a series of automated weather stations that are installed around the Bay Area with the purpose of monitoring local weather phenomena such as fog dynamics. Unfortunately, many of these stations are not currently active.

4.1.2. California Air Resources Board (CARB) Network

Meteorological measurements are taken at CARB sites in support of their overall mission of promoting and protecting public health, welfare and ecological resources in California through the reduction of air pollutants, while accounting for economical effects of such measures. Measured elements include temperature, relative humidity, precipitation, and wind speed and direction.

4.1.3. Clean Air Status and Trends Network (CASTNet)

CASTNet is primarily an air-quality monitoring network managed by the EPA. Standard hourly weather and climate elements are measured and include temperature, wind, humidity, solar radiation, soil temperature, and sometimes moisture. These elements are intended to support interpretation of air-quality parameters that also are measured at CASTNet sites. Data records at CASTNet sites are generally one–two decades in length.

4.1.4. California Irrigation Management Information System (CIMIS)

The California Irrigation Management Information System (CIMIS), operated through the California Department of Water Resources (CDWR), is a network of over 120 automated weather stations in the state of California. CIMIS stations are used to assist irrigators in managing their water resources efficiently. Measured meteorological elements at CIMIS stations generally include temperature, precipitation, wind, and solar radiation. Some stations measure additional parameters such as soil temperature and moisture.

4.1.5. NWS Cooperative Observer Program (COOP)

The COOP network has been a foundation of the U.S. climate program for decades and continues to play an important role. Manual measurements are made by volunteers and consist of daily maximum and minimum temperatures, observation-time temperature, daily precipitation, daily snowfall, and snow depth. When blended with NWS measurements, the data set is known as SOD, or "Summary of the Day." The quality of data from COOP sites ranges from excellent to modest.

4.1.6. Citizen Weather Observer Program (CWOP)

The CWOP network consists primarily of automated weather stations operated by private citizens who have either an Internet connection and/or a wireless Ham radio setup. Data from CWOP stations are specifically intended for use in research, education, and homeland security activities. Although standard meteorological elements such as temperature, precipitation, and wind are measured at all CWOP stations, station characteristics do vary, including sensor types and site exposure.

4.1.7. Desert Research Institute (DRI) Network

The Desert Research Institute (DRI) operates this network of automated weather stations, located primarily in California and Western Nevada. Many of these stations are located in remote mountain and desert locations and provide data that are often used in support of various mountain- and desert-based environmental studies in the region. Meteorology elements are measured every 10 minutes and include temperature, wind, humidity, barometric pressure, precipitation, and solar radiation.

4.1.8. Gaseous Pollutant Monitoring Program (GPMP)

The GPMP network, managed by NPS, measures hourly meteorological data in support of pollutant monitoring activities. Measured elements include temperature, precipitation, humidity, wind, solar radiation, and surface wetness. These data are generally of high quality, with records extending up to two decades in length.

4.1.9. National Atmospheric Deposition Program (NADP)

The purpose of the NADP network is to monitor primarily wet deposition at selected sites around the U.S. and its territories. The network is a collaborative effort among several agencies including USDA and the United States Geological Survey (USGS). Precipitation is the primary climate parameter measured at NADP sites.

4.1.10. USDA/NRCS Snowcourse Network (NRCS-SC)

The USDA/NRCS maintains a network of snow-monitoring stations in addition to SNOTEL (described below). These sites are known as snowcourses. These are all manual sites, measuring only snow depth and snow water content one–two times per month during the months of January to June. Data records for these snowcourses often extend back to the 1920s or 1930s, and the data are generally of high quality. Many of these sites have been replaced by SNOTEL sites, but several hundred snowcourses are still in operation.

4.1.11. Portable Ozone Monitoring System (POMS)

The POMS network is operated by the NPS Air Resources Division. Sites are intended primarily for summer, short-term (1-5 years) monitoring of near-surface atmospheric ozone levels in remote locations. Measured meteorological elements include temperature, precipitation, wind, relative humidity, and solar radiation.

4.1.12. Remote Automated Weather Station Network (RAWS)

The RAWS network is administered through many land management agencies, particularly the BLM and the Forest Service. Hourly meteorology elements are measured and include temperature, wind, humidity, solar radiation, barometric pressure, fuel temperature, and precipitation (when temperatures are above freezing). The fire community is the primary client for RAWS data. These sites are remote and data typically are transmitted via GOES (Geostationary Operational Environmental Satellite). Some sites operate all winter. Most data records for RAWS sites began during or after the mid-1980s.

4.1.13. NWS Surface Airways Observation (SAO) Network

These stations are located usually at major airports and military bases. Almost all SAO sites are automated. The hourly data measured at these sites include temperature, precipitation, humidity, wind, barometric pressure, sky cover, ceiling, visibility, and current weather. Most data records begin during or after the 1940s, and these data are generally of high quality.

4.1.14. USDA/NRCS Snowfall Telemetry (SNOTEL) Network

The USDA/NRCS maintains a network of automated snow-monitoring stations known as SNOTEL. The network was implemented originally to measure daily precipitation and snow water content. Many modern SNOTEL sites now record hourly data, with some sites now recording temperature and snow depth. Most data records began during or after the mid-1970s.

4.1.15. University of California Santa Barbara (UCSB) Network

These stations are maintained and operated by UCSB's Donald Bren School of Environmental Science and Management, which runs several research projects in SIEN park units. The parameters measured at these sites generally include air temperature, precipitation, humidity, wind, and solar radiation.

UCSB also helps operate the Mammoth Mountain Energy Balance Monitoring Site (http://neige.bren.ucsb.edu/mmsa), in collaboration with Mammoth Mountain Ski Area, the National Aeronautics and Space Administration (NASA) and the U.S. Army Corps of Engineers (USACE) Cold Regions Research and Engineering Laboratory (CRREL). This site provides valuable weather observations for both DEPO and YOSE. Data access was not verified for the station at the time of this report.

4.1.16. Weather For You Network (WX4U)
The WX4U network is a nationwide collection of weather stations run by local observers. Data quality varies with site. Standard meteorological elements are measured and usually include temperature, precipitation, wind, and humidity.

4.1.17. California Data Exchange Center (CDEC)
Some stations are identified in this report as CDEC stations. This is a data repository for a number of California stations from a variety of federal and state agencies. Measured meteorological elements vary widely depending on agency. Data from CDEC stations are usually hourly.

Included in CDEC are many CDWR stations, including the California Cooperative Snow Survey (CSS) network. The CSS was established to address a state mandate that the CDWR collect snowpack, precipitation, and streamflow data in order to forecast seasonal runoff. These forecasts are used by various utilities and agricultural groups in the state of California. We identified from these agencies additional stations that are not in CDEC. These stations are listed in Appendix H.

4.1.18. Weather Bureau Army Navy (WBAN)
Some stations are identified in this report as WBAN stations. This is a station identification system rather than a true weather/climate network. Stations identified with WBAN are largely historical stations that reported meteorological observations on the WBAN weather observation forms that were common during the early and middle parts of the twentieth century. The use of WBAN numbers to identify stations was one of the first attempts in the U.S. to use a coordinated station numbering scheme between several weather station networks, such as the COOP and SAO networks.

4.1.19. Other Networks
In addition to the major networks mentioned above, there are various networks that are operated for specific purposes by specific organizations or governmental agencies or scientific research projects. These networks could be present within SIEN but have not been identified in this report. Some of the commonly used networks include the following:

- NOAA upper-air stations
- Federal and state departments of transportation
- U.S. Department of Energy Surface Radiation Budget Network (Surfrad)
- Park-specific-monitoring networks and stations
- Other research or project networks having many possible owners

In addition, USACE stations were identified for SIEN park units. However, data access for these stations could not be verified at the time of this report, so these stations are listed in Appendix H.

4.2. Station Locations
The major weather and climate networks in the SIEN (discussed in Section 4.1) have at most several stations at or inside each park unit (Table 4.2). Most of these are COOP stations.

Table 4.2. Number of stations within or nearby SIEN park units. Numbers are listed by park unit and by weather/climate network. Figures in parentheses indicate the numbers of stations within park boundaries.

Network	DEPO	SEKI	YOSE
BAMI	0(0)	1(0)	2(0)
CARB	0(0)	4(2)	4(3)
CASTNet	0(0)	3(2)	1(1)
CIMIS	0(0)	7(0)	8(0)
COOP	16(0)	89(23)	76(16)
CWOP	3(0)	6(0)	16(1)
DRI	0(0)	17(0)	4(1)
GPMP	0(0)	5(5)	5(4)
NADP	0(0)	2(1)	1(1)
NRCS-SC	1(0)	0(0)	8(0)
POMS	1(0)	0(0)	1(1)
RAWS	8(1)	25(7)	28(5)
SAO	1(0)	2(0)	1(0)
SNOTEL	0(0)	0(0)	7(0)
UCSB	0(0)	4(4)	0(0)
WX4U	0(0)	1(0)	0(0)
Other	15(1)	29(11)	34(8)
Total	45(2)	195(55)	196(41)

Lists of stations have been compiled for the SIEN. As noted previously, a station does not have to be within the boundaries to provide useful data and information regarding the park unit in question. Some might be physically *within* the administrative or political boundaries, whereas others might be just outside, or even some distance away, but would be *nearby* in behavior and representativeness. What constitutes "useful" and "representative" are also significant questions, whose answers can vary according to application, type of element, period of record, procedural or methodological observation conventions, and the like.

4.2.1. Devils Postpile National Monument
One active weather station, "Devils Postpile," was identified within the boundaries of DEPO (Table 4.3; Figure 4.1). The operation and maintenance of this site is a collaborative effort between NPS, CDWR, the Scripps Institution of Oceanography, and the USGS. It has only become operational since September 2006 and data are available through CDEC. Thirteen other stations that provide data through the CDEC system are active within 40 km of DEPO. Many of these CDEC stations are CSS stations, providing information on temperature and precipitation (rain and snow).

28

Table 4.3. Weather and climate stations for DEPO. Stations inside DEPO and within 40 km of the park unit boundary are included. Missing entries are indicated by "M".

Devils Postpile National Monument (DEPO)

Name	Lat.	Lon.	Elev. (m)	Network	Start	End	In Park?
Devils Postpile	37.629	-119.085	2305	NPS	9/1/2006	Present	Yes
Devils Post Pile	37.630	-119.093	2304	RAWS	11/1/1993	8/31/2004	Yes
Agnew Pass	37.728	-119.143	2880	CDEC	10/1/1989	Present	No
Dana Meadows	37.897	-119.257	2987	CDEC	10/1/1985	Present	No
Ellery Lake	37.933	-119.233	2940	CDEC	11/1/2002	Present	No
Gem Pass	37.780	-119.170	3277	CDEC	10/1/1985	Present	No
Graveyard Meadow	37.465	-119.290	2103	CDEC	7/1/1998	Present	No
Green Mountain	37.555	-119.238	2408	CDEC	7/1/1998	Present	No
Kaiser Point	37.300	-119.100	2804	CDEC	9/1/1998	Present	No
Mammoth Pass (USBR)	37.610	-119.033	2835	CDEC	9/1/1998	Present	No
Rock Creek Lakes	37.455	-118.743	3048	CDEC	1/1/1986	Present	No
Tenaya Lake	37.838	-119.448	2484	CDEC	10/1/1998	Present	No
Tioga Pass Entry Stn.	37.911	-119.257	3031	CDEC	2/1/2002	Present	No
Tuolumne Meadows (DWR)	37.873	-119.350	2621	CDEC	10/1/1985	Present	No
Volcanic Knob	37.388	-118.903	3063	CDEC	8/1/1989	Present	No
Chiquito Creek	37.500	-119.383	2223	COOP	9/1/1961	9/30/1976	No
Clover Meadows G.S.	37.533	-119.283	2135	COOP	7/1/1948	11/30/1972	No
Ellery Lake	37.936	-119.231	2940	COOP	11/1/1924	12/27/2006	No
Florence Lake	37.274	-118.973	2233	COOP	7/1/1948	Present	No
Gem Lake	37.752	-119.140	2734	COOP	11/1/1924	12/27/2006	No
Kaiser Meadows	37.300	-119.100	2779	COOP	7/1/1948	9/30/1976	No
Lee Vining	37.957	-119.119	2072	COOP	4/15/1988	Present	No
Mammoth Lakes R.S.	37.648	-118.962	2379	COOP	12/1/1993	Present	No
Mammoth Pass	37.617	-119.033	2861	COOP	7/1/1948	9/30/1976	No
Mammoth Pool	37.350	-119.317	1034	COOP	7/23/1947	9/30/1976	No
Mt. Givens	37.283	-119.083	2898	COOP	10/1/1963	4/1/1969	No
Rock Creek	37.450	-118.733	2949	COOP	7/1/1948	9/30/1976	No
Rose Marie Meadow	37.317	-118.867	3050	COOP	10/1/1953	9/30/1976	No
Rush Creek Ranch	37.950	-119.067	1967	COOP	7/1/1948	10/31/1950	No
Tuolumne Meadows	37.883	-119.350	2638	COOP	7/1/1948	11/30/1972	No
Vermilion Valley	37.367	-118.983	2294	COOP	12/1/1946	9/30/1976	No
CW2998 Mammoth Lakes	37.651	-118.976	2500	CWOP	M	Present	No
CW4849 Crowley Lake	37.564	-118.742	2105	CWOP	M	Present	No
CW5780 Lee Vining	37.956	-119.120	2067	CWOP	M	Present	No
Lee Vining Hill	37.965	-119.146	2715	M	M	Present	No
Tioga Pass	37.917	-119.250	3018	NRCS-SC	1/1/1926	Present	No
Tioga Pass	37.911	-119.259	3037	POMS	7/20/2005	Present	No
Crestview	37.745	-118.983	2316	RAWS	11/1/1993	Present	No
Gaylor Meadow	37.868	-119.318	2825	RAWS	8/1/1988	Present	No

Devils Postpile National Monument (DEPO)

Name	Lat.	Lon.	Elev. (m)	Network	Start	End	In Park?
High Sierra	37.315	-119.038	2256	RAWS	7/1/2001	Present	No
Minarets	37.407	-119.346	1628	RAWS	12/1/2004	Present	No
Mono Lake - Portable	37.688	-118.981	2187	RAWS	6/1/1995	12/31/1995	No
Mount Tom	37.376	-119.178	2749	RAWS	8/1/1999	7/31/2005	No
Rock Creek	37.551	-118.667	2146	RAWS	6/1/1999	Present	No
Mammoth Yosemite Arpt.	37.633	-118.850	2173	SAO	2/1/1973	Present	No

Besides "Devils Postpile," the closest CDEC station to DEPO is "Mammoth Pass (USBR)," which is 5 km southeast of DEPO. A weather station was identified at Lee Vining Hill, 37 km north of DEPO. The NRCS-SC and POMS sites at Tioga Pass are 34 km northwest of DEPO.

We identified 16 COOP stations within 40 km of DEPO (Table 4.3). Only three of these stations are active. Two additional stations, "Ellery Lake" and "Gem Lake," indicate end dates in late December of 2006. These two stations may very well still be active; both have data records going back to 1924 and thus may provide useful long-term climate records for DEPO. The COOP station "Florence Lake" is 37 km south of DEPO; unfortunately, its data record is unreliable. The closest active COOP station to DEPO is "Mammoth Lakes R.S.," which is 11 km east of the park unit. This station has been operating since 1993. The COOP station "Lee Vining," 36 km north of DEPO, has been operating since 1988.

The SAO station "Mammoth Yosemite Arpt." is a source of near-real-time data for DEPO, situated 21 km east of the park unit (Figure 4.1). This site has had occasional data gaps throughout its data record (1973-2006). The last such gap occurred in March and April of 2006. Eight RAWS stations (five active) provide additional sources of near-real-time weather data for DEPO (Table 4.3). Most of these RAWS stations are at least 15 km from DEPO; however, the RAWS station "Devils Post Pile," which operated until 2004, was inside DEPO. Reliable data records are found at the RAWS sites "Crestview" (1993-present), 15 km northeast of DEPO, and "High Sierra" (2001-present), 32 km south of DEPO. The RAWS station "Minarets" (2004-present), 31 km south of DEPO, has provided data reliably since June 2005. The RAWS station "Gaylor Meadow" (1988-present), 33 km northwest of DEPO, has had scattered data gaps in its record but has been quite reliable since August 2000. The RAWS station "Rock Creek" (1999-present) is 37 km southeast of DEPO.

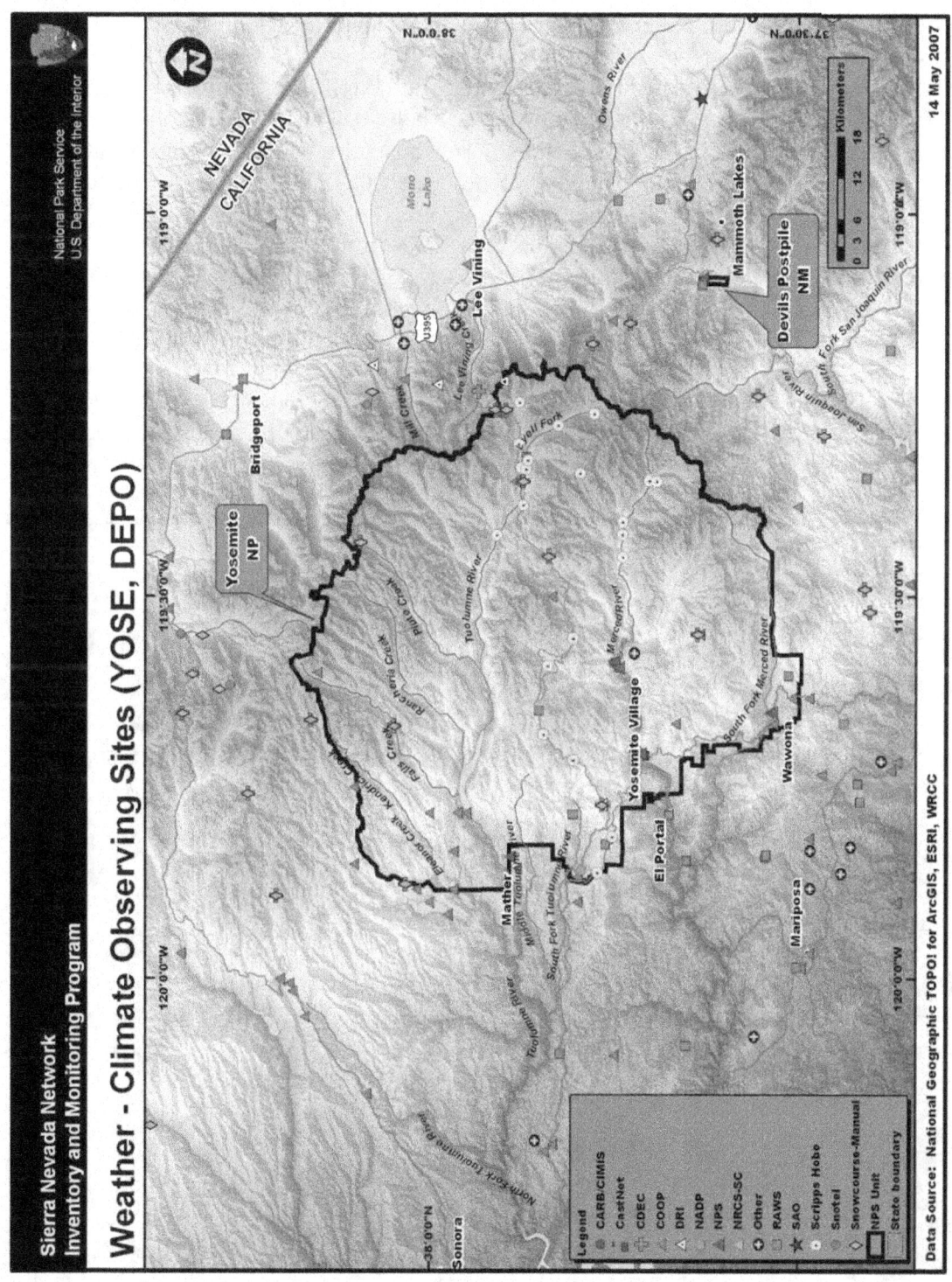

Figure 4.1. Station locations for DEPO and YOSE.

4.2.2. Yosemite National Park

We identified 41 stations within YOSE, 22 of which are active (Table 4.4). Most of these stations are located either in western YOSE or along Tioga Road (Figure 4.1). Three CARB stations are currently operating inside YOSE. Two of these stations, "Yosemite NP-Merced River" and "Yosemite Village-Visitor Center," are located in Yosemite Village. A third CARB station is located at Turtleback Dome in southwest YOSE; a CASTNet site is also located at Turtleback Dome and has been operating since 1994. Eight stations that provide data through the CDEC system were identified within YOSE. Only one of these stations is not active; this station, "Gin Flat" (1985-2002), was located in western YOSE (although monitoring efforts have been continued at the DRI station "Gin Flat TC Tower;" see below). Three COOP stations are currently active within YOSE. The COOP station "Hetch Hetchy" (1910-present), located in northwestern YOSE, has a very complete data record. The COOP station "South Entrance Yosemite" is in extreme southern YOSE and has a data record that goes back to 1941. With the exception of large gaps from January 1971 to March 1972, from March to April of 1973, and in January 2004, the data record at "South Entrance Yosemite" is quite complete. The COOP station "Yosemite Park Hq." is at Yosemite Village and has a data record going back to 1905. This site's record is largely complete, with scattered, small data gaps throughout.

Table 4.4. Weather and climate stations for YOSE. Stations inside YOSE and within 40 km of the park unit boundary are included. Missing entries are indicated by "M".

Yosemite National Park (YOSE)							
Name	Lat.	Lon.	Elev. (m)	Network	Start	End	In Park?
Yosemite NP-Merced River	37.743	-119.594	1220	CARB	M	Present	Yes
Yosemite NP-Turtleback Dome	37.711	-119.706	1611	CARB	M	Present	Yes
Yosemite Village-Visitor Center.	37.749	-119.587	1213	CARB	M	Present	Yes
Turtleback Dome	37.713	-119.706	1605	CASTNet	1/1/1994	Present	Yes
Dana Meadows	37.897	-119.257	2987	CDEC	10/1/1985	Present	Yes
Gin Flat	37.767	-119.773	2149	CDEC	10/1/1985	10/31/2002	Yes
Lower Kibbie Ridge	38.032	-119.877	2042	CDEC	10/1/1985	Present	Yes
Ostrander Lake	37.637	-119.550	2499	CDEC	10/1/1988	Present	Yes
Paradise Meadow	38.047	-119.670	2332	CDEC	10/1/1985	Present	Yes
Slide Canyon	38.092	-119.430	2804	CDEC	10/1/1985	Present	Yes
Tenaya Lake	37.838	-119.448	2484	CDEC	10/1/1998	Present	Yes
Tuolumne Mdws. (DWR)	37.873	-119.350	2621	CDEC	10/1/1985	Present	Yes
Badger Pass	37.667	-119.667	2227	COOP	7/1/1948	6/30/1976	Yes
Beehive Meadow	38.000	-119.783	1983	COOP	7/1/1948	9/30/1971	Yes
Grace Meadow	38.150	-119.600	2715	COOP	7/1/1948	6/30/1973	Yes
Hetch Hetchy	37.961	-119.783	1180	COOP	10/1/1910	Present	Yes
Hodgdon Meadow	37.800	-119.867	1281	COOP	6/1/1967	6/30/1978	Yes
Lake Eleanor	37.967	-119.883	1421	COOP	10/19/1909	2/28/1973	Yes
Miguel Meadows	37.967	-119.833	1617	COOP	11/1/1946	6/30/1948	Yes
Oshaughnessy Dam	37.950	-119.783	1220	COOP	11/1/1946	5/5/1948	Yes
Ostrander Lake	37.633	-119.550	2623	COOP	7/1/1948	9/30/1976	Yes

Yosemite National Park (YOSE)

Name	Lat.	Lon.	Elev. (m)	Network	Start	End	In Park?
Paradise Meadow	38.050	-119.667	2349	COOP	8/1/1948	9/30/1971	Yes
Snow Flat	37.833	-119.500	2654	COOP	7/1/1948	9/30/1976	Yes
South Entrance Yosemite	37.508	-119.634	1566	COOP	7/1/1941	Present	Yes
Tuolumne Meadows	37.883	-119.350	2638	COOP	7/1/1948	11/30/1972	Yes
Wawona	37.533	-119.667	1190	COOP	1/1/1934	6/30/1941	Yes
Wawona R.S.	37.540	-119.652	1215	COOP	10/1/1940	6/15/2006	Yes
Yosemite Park Hq.	37.750	-119.590	1209	COOP	1/12/1905	Present	Yes
K6IXA-2 Yosemite Park	37.723	-119.575	2469	CWOP	M	Present	Yes
Gin Flat TC Tower	37.767	-119.773	2149	DRI	10/1/2003	Present	Yes
Merced River	37.743	-119.594	1219	GPMP	8/1/2002	12/31/2005	Yes
Turtleback Dome	37.713	-119.706	1605	GPMP	1/1/1992	12/1/1992	Yes
Wawona Valley	37.536	-119.652	1220	GPMP	4/1/1987	10/1/1996	Yes
Yosemite Valley	37.750	-119.587	1219	GPMP	12/1/1989	11/30/1994	Yes
Yosemite NP-Hodgdon Meadow	37.796	-119.858	1408	NADP	12/8/1981	Present	Yes
Tioga Pass	37.911	-119.259	3037	POMS	7/20/2005	Present	Yes
Crane Flat Lookout	37.762	-119.825	2025	RAWS	11/1/1991	Present	Yes
Gaylor Meadow	37.868	-119.318	2825	RAWS	8/1/1988	Present	Yes
Golden Gate NRA #2	37.806	-119.785	1829	RAWS	6/1/1994	10/31/1998	Yes
Mariposa Grove	37.513	-119.605	1951	RAWS	9/1/1988	Present	Yes
White Wolf	37.851	-119.650	2446	RAWS	8/1/1988	Present	Yes
Five Mile Learning Center	38.049	-120.300	114	CARB	M	Present	No
Jerseydale-6440 Jerseydale	37.545	-119.842	1143	CARB	M	Present	No
Agnew Pass	37.728	-119.143	2880	CDEC	10/1/1989	Present	No
Bishop Pass	37.100	-118.557	3414	CDEC	1/1/1988	Present	No
Chilkoot Meadow	37.410	-119.490	2179	CDEC	7/1/1998	Present	No
Deadman Creek	38.332	-119.653	2819	CDEC	9/1/1987	Present	No
Ellery Lake	37.933	-119.233	2940	CDEC	11/1/2002	Present	No
Gem Pass	37.780	-119.170	3277	CDEC	10/1/1985	Present	No
Gianelli Meadow	38.205	-119.892	2560	CDEC	9/1/1998	Present	No
Graveyard Meadow	37.465	-119.290	2103	CDEC	7/1/1998	Present	No
Green Mountain	37.555	-119.238	2408	CDEC	7/1/1998	Present	No
Highland Meadow	38.490	-119.805	2408	CDEC	10/1/1989	Present	No
Horse Meadow	38.158	-119.662	2560	CDEC	10/1/1985	Present	No
Huntington Lake (USBR)	37.228	-119.221	2134	CDEC	7/1/1998	Present	No
Kaiser Point	37.300	-119.100	2804	CDEC	9/1/1998	Present	No
Lower Relief Valley	38.243	-119.758	2469	CDEC	10/1/1985	Present	No
Mammoth Pass (USBR)	37.610	-119.033	2835	CDEC	9/1/1998	Present	No
Poison Ridge	37.403	-119.520	2103	CDEC	7/1/1998	Present	No
Tioga Pass Entry Stn.	37.911	-119.257	3031	CDEC	2/1/2002	Present	No
Ahwahnee	37.367	-119.717	708	COOP	2/1/1957	3/31/1959	No
Ahwahnee	37.374	-119.728	850	COOP	12/1/1960	11/30/2005	No

Yosemite National Park (YOSE)

Name	Lat.	Lon.	Elev. (m)	Network	Start	End	In Park?
Big Creek PH 1	37.206	-119.242	1487	COOP	6/1/1915	Present	No
Bodie	38.212	-119.014	2551	COOP	2/1/1895	Present	No
Bridgeport	38.258	-119.229	1972	COOP	10/1/1903	Present	No
Bridgeport Dam	38.317	-119.217	1958	COOP	4/1/1925	6/30/1957	No
Bridgeport R.S.	38.251	-119.216	1963	COOP	6/1/1950	Present	No
Bumblebee Trailer P.A.	38.200	-120.000	1757	COOP	2/1/1964	11/30/1964	No
Catheys Vly. Bull Run Rch.	37.400	-120.050	436	COOP	7/1/1948	5/31/1977	No
Cedar Point Ranch	37.467	-119.733	985	COOP	6/1/1959	6/30/1962	No
Central Camp	37.350	-119.483	1635	COOP	12/1/1923	12/31/1948	No
Cherry Valley Camp	38.000	-119.900	1373	COOP	11/1/1946	6/22/1948	No
Cherry Valley Dam	37.975	-119.916	1452	COOP	10/1/1955	Present	No
Chiquito Creek	37.500	-119.383	2223	COOP	9/1/1961	9/30/1976	No
Clover Meadows G.S.	37.533	-119.283	2135	COOP	7/1/1948	11/30/1972	No
Coarsegold 1 SW	37.250	-119.705	680	COOP	2/6/1957	Present	No
Cold Springs Chalet	38.167	-120.050	1751	COOP	2/1/1951	8/31/1953	No
Coleville	38.513	-119.449	1696	COOP	4/19/1983	Present	No
Coleville 3 SE	38.533	-119.467	1617	COOP	2/1/1945	7/31/1946	No
Coleville 4 SE	38.517	-119.467	1617	COOP	5/1/1949	1/31/1953	No
Crocker Stn.	37.800	-119.900	1434	COOP	1/17/1904	10/31/1953	No
Donnells Dam	38.333	-119.967	1476	COOP	6/1/1959	10/31/1960	No
Dudleys	37.750	-120.100	915	COOP	8/1/1908	10/31/1976	No
Ellery Lake	37.936	-119.231	2940	COOP	11/1/1924	12/27/2006	No
Fish Camp	37.483	-119.633	1562	COOP	5/1/1971	3/31/1972	No
Gem Lake	37.752	-119.140	2734	COOP	11/1/1924	12/27/2006	No
Groveland	37.833	-120.217	854	COOP	1/1/1905	12/31/1954	No
Groveland 2	37.844	-120.226	853	COOP	7/1/1948	Present	No
Groveland R.S.	37.823	-120.098	959	COOP	10/1/1906	Present	No
Highland Lakes	38.500	-119.800	2638	COOP	7/1/1961	9/30/1976	No
Huckleberry Lake	38.100	-119.750	2379	COOP	8/1/1948	9/30/1971	No
Huntington Lake	37.228	-119.221	2140	COOP	6/1/1915	Present	No
Kaiser Meadows	37.300	-119.100	2779	COOP	7/1/1948	9/30/1976	No
Lee Vining	37.957	-119.119	2072	COOP	4/15/1988	Present	No
Long Barn 1 W	38.083	-120.150	1491	COOP	9/1/1965	12/31/1978	No
Long Barn Exp.	38.183	-120.017	1586	COOP	7/1/1948	2/28/1964	No
Lower Kibbey Ridge	38.017	-119.883	1983	COOP	1/1/1949	9/30/1971	No
Lundy Lake	38.033	-119.217	2367	COOP	1/1/1931	5/31/1940	No
Mammoth Lakes R.S.	37.648	-118.962	2379	COOP	12/1/1993	Present	No
Mammoth Pass	37.617	-119.033	2861	COOP	7/1/1948	9/30/1976	No
Mammoth Pool	37.350	-119.317	1034	COOP	7/23/1947	9/30/1976	No
Mariposa	37.483	-119.967	613	COOP	1/1/1893	9/18/1984	No
Mariposa R.S.	37.495	-119.986	640	COOP	5/1/1953	Present	No
Mather	37.881	-119.856	1375	COOP	10/9/1947	Present	No

Yosemite National Park (YOSE)

Name	Lat.	Lon.	Elev. (m)	Network	Start	End	In Park?
Mono Lake	38.000	-119.150	1966	COOP	5/1/1943	3/30/1988	No
Mt. Givens	37.283	-119.083	2898	COOP	10/1/1963	4/1/1969	No
North Fork R.S.	37.231	-119.507	802	COOP	3/1/1904	Present	No
Oakhurst	37.331	-119.653	680	COOP	10/1/1999	Present	No
Penon Blanco	37.733	-120.267	854	COOP	5/1/1953	Present	No
Pickel Meadows	38.350	-119.517	2074	COOP	6/1/1959	9/30/1959	No
Pinecrest Summit R.S.	38.187	-120.006	1707	COOP	11/27/1964	Present	No
Raymond	37.210	-119.908	288	COOP	2/1/1957	Present	No
Raymond 10 N	37.350	-119.867	390	COOP	2/21/1962	2/9/1966	No
Raymond Whipple Ranch	37.367	-119.900	421	COOP	8/1/1959	2/28/1962	No
Rush Creek Ranch	37.950	-119.067	1967	COOP	7/1/1948	10/31/1950	No
Saches Springs	38.100	-119.850	2410	COOP	9/1/1948	9/30/1971	No
Shields Ranch	38.533	-119.517	1684	COOP	1/1/1931	5/31/1946	No
Sonora Junction	38.351	-119.450	2099	COOP	9/1/1959	Present	No
Usona 2 N	37.483	-119.817	961	COOP	3/1/1972	11/4/1980	No
Wishon P.H.	37.150	-119.500	305	COOP	12/1/1957	12/31/1978	No
CW1522 Mariposa	37.429	-119.828	838	CWOP	M	Present	No
CW2959 Ahwahnee	37.388	-119.716	837	CWOP	M	Present	No
CW2998 Mammoth Lakes	37.651	-118.976	2500	CWOP	M	Present	No
CW3161 Sonora	37.916	-120.283	732	CWOP	M	Present	No
CW3491 Mariposa	37.483	-119.833	1011	CWOP	M	Present	No
CW3796 Bass Lake	37.321	-119.563	1044	CWOP	M	Present	No
CW4249 Lee Vining	38.042	-119.142	2080	CWOP	M	Present	No
CW4289 Lockwood	38.498	-120.563	1067	CWOP	M	Present	No
CW4643 Lee Vining	38.034	-119.170	2164	CWOP	M	Present	No
CW4962 Mariposa	37.483	-119.883	2750	CWOP	M	Present	No
CW5780 Lee Vining	37.956	-119.120	2067	CWOP	M	Present	No
KE6KYI Groveland	37.858	-120.212	762	CWOP	M	Present	No
KG6QHD Sonora	38.002	-120.297	839	CWOP	M	Present	No
NM6G Mariposa	37.442	-119.863	635	CWOP	M	Present	No
W6BXN-3 Bear Valley	37.560	-120.076	1280	CWOP	M	Present	No
Conway Ridge	38.076	-119.198	2691	DRI	9/1/1995	6/30/2004	No
Conway Ridge (Hourly)	38.076	-119.198	2691	DRI	9/1/1995	4/30/1996	No
Mt. Warren	37.990	-119.224	3757	DRI	7/1/2006	Present	No
Camp Mather	37.891	-119.841	1445	GPMP	2/1/1988	8/1/1996	No
Lee Vining Hill	37.965	-119.146	2715	M	M	Present	No
Center Mountain	38.150	-119.467	2865	NRCS-SC	1/1/1922	Present	No
Leavitt Lake	38.276	-119.612	2931	NRCS-SC	1/1/1981	Present	No
Sawmill Ridge	38.183	-119.350	2667	NRCS-SC	1/1/1976	Present	No
Sonora Pass	38.317	-119.600	2682	NRCS-SC	1/1/1932	Present	No
Tioga Pass	37.917	-119.250	3018	NRCS-SC	1/1/1926	Present	No
Virginia Lakes	38.083	-119.250	2896	NRCS-SC	1/1/1947	Present	No

Yosemite National Park (YOSE)

Name	Lat.	Lon.	Elev. (m)	Network	Start	End	In Park?
Virginia Lakes Ridge	38.083	-119.250	2804	NRCS-SC	1/1/1969	Present	No
Willow Flat	38.267	-119.450	2515	NRCS-SC	1/1/1925	Present	No
Batterson	37.232	-119.508	963	RAWS	9/1/1999	Present	No
Bridgeport	38.272	-119.289	1975	RAWS	6/1/2002	6/30/2005	No
Bridgeport 4 NW	38.272	-119.289	2027	RAWS	11/1/2002	Present	No
Buck Meadows	37.823	-120.098	975	RAWS	5/1/1999	Present	No
Canon BAER (Shingle)	38.445	-119.470	2256	RAWS	11/1/2002	Present	No
Catheys Valley	37.468	-120.111	366	RAWS	1/1/1999	Present	No
Crestview	37.745	-118.983	2316	RAWS	11/1/1993	Present	No
Devils Post Pile	37.630	-119.093	2304	RAWS	11/1/1993	8/31/2004	No
El Portal	37.676	-119.786	625	RAWS	6/1/2004	7/31/2005	No
Golden Gate NRA #3	37.652	-119.846	139	RAWS	9/1/1995	8/31/1999	No
Jerseydale	37.544	-119.839	1189	RAWS	6/1/2002	Present	No
Mariposa	37.501	-119.985	693	RAWS	5/1/1990	Present	No
Merced River	37.653	-120.088	792	RAWS	10/1/1991	11/30/1997	No
Metcalf Gap	37.416	-119.769	1006	RAWS	5/1/1990	Present	No
Miami	37.419	-119.745	1321	RAWS	12/1/2004	Present	No
Minarets	37.407	-119.346	1628	RAWS	12/1/2004	Present	No
Mono Lake - Portable	37.688	-118.981	2187	RAWS	6/1/1995	12/31/1995	No
Mount Elizabeth	38.063	-120.247	1504	RAWS	7/1/1999	Present	No
Mount Tom	37.376	-119.178	2749	RAWS	8/1/1999	7/31/2005	No
North Fork	37.233	-119.505	829	RAWS	8/1/1998	Present	No
North Fork Portable	37.438	-119.666	1737	RAWS	M	Present	No
Toiyabe Portable FTS	38.250	-119.217	1968	RAWS	12/1/1998	10/31/1999	No
Trench 1	38.161	-118.911	2073	RAWS	1/1/1998	1/31/2002	No
Mammoth Yosemite Arpt.	37.633	-118.850	2173	SAO	2/1/1973	Present	No
Leavitt Lake	38.267	-119.617	2865	SNOTEL	10/1/1989	Present	No
Leavitt Meadows	38.333	-119.550	2195	SNOTEL	10/1/1980	Present	No
Lobdell Lake	38.433	-119.367	2804	SNOTEL	10/1/1978	Present	No
Poison Flat	38.500	-119.633	2408	SNOTEL	10/1/1980	Present	No
Sonora Pass	38.317	-119.600	2682	SNOTEL	10/1/1978	Present	No
Summit Meadow	38.400	-119.517	2780	SNOTEL	9/20/2003	Present	No
Virginia Lakes Ridge	38.083	-119.250	2804	SNOTEL	10/1/1978	Present	No

The DRI station "Gin Flat TC Tower" has been operating at Gin Flats in western YOSE since 2003 (Table 4.4; Figure 4.1). Also located in western YOSE is the NADP station "Yosemite NP-Hodgdon" (1981-present), located at the Highway 120 entrance into YOSE. On the other side of the park unit, a POMS station has been active at Tioga Pass since 2005.

Five RAWS stations were identified within YOSE (Table 4.4). All of the active RAWS stations in YOSE (four) have fairly lengthy data records for RAWS stations, each approaching two decades in length. "Crane Flat Lookout" (1991-present) is in western YOSE but has not had data since May 2006. "Gaylor Meadow" (1988-present), discussed previously, is in eastern YOSE. "Mariposa Grove" (1988-present), in southern YOSE, had occasional data gaps until October 1998 but has had a very complete data record since that time. "White Wolf" (1988-present), which is in central YOSE along Tioga Road, has had scattered, small gaps throughout its data record.

Two CARB sites were identified within 40 km of the boundaries of YOSE (Table 4.4). "Five Mile Learning Center" is 37 km west of YOSE and "Jerseydale-6440 Jerseydale" is 12 km southwest of YOSE.

Seventeen stations that provide data through the CDEC system are active within 40 km of the boundaries of YOSE. Many of these CDEC stations are California Department of Water Resources sites or California Cooperative Snow Survey sites.

We identified 60 COOP stations, 20 of which are active, within 40 km of the boundaries of YOSE (Table 4.4; Figure 4.1). Six active COOP stations have data records that go back to the 1910s or earlier. The COOP station "Big Creek PH 1," 40 km southeast of YOSE, has been active since 1915. The data record at this site is unreliable for climate-monitoring purposes, with a large gap extending from the early 1960s through the late 1990s. The COOP station "Bodie," 32 km northeast of YOSE, has been active since 1895, providing the longest data record of the active COOP stations near YOSE. However, the data record at this site has only become reliable since the early 1960s. The COOP station "Bridgeport" is 22 km northeast of YOSE and has been active since 1903. Numerous data gaps occurred in the data record at "Bridgeport" up until 1957; after that time, the data record has become much more reliable, with only occasional, small data gaps. The COOP station "Groveland R.S." is located 20 km west of YOSE and has been operating since 1906. This site has mainly measured precipitation and its data record is largely complete after 1955, with scattered data gaps. The COOP station "Huntington Lake" is located 39 km southeast of YOSE and has been operating since 1915. While the temperature record at this site is largely complete (with only scattered small data gaps), the precipitation record had a significant gap throughout the 1960s and early 1970s. The COOP station "North Fork R.S." is located 30 km south of YOSE and has been operating since 1904. This site's data record has been quite reliable during the summer months. "North Fork R.S." generally does not have weekend observations, especially during the winter months. Several other COOP stations within 40 km of YOSE have data records extending back to the 1950s or earlier.

Several weather and climate networks have been identified that currently provide near-real-time data for the region surrounding YOSE. Fifteen CWOP stations were identified within 40 km of YOSE boundaries (Table 4.4). Most of these are located in communities south and west of the park unit; however, CWOP stations were also identified in the communities of Lee Vining and Mammoth Lakes, east of YOSE (Figure 4.1). The DRI network of weather stations currently has one active station within 40 km of YOSE. "Mount Warren" has been obtaining near-real-time weather data since July 2006 from the summit of Mount Warren, 8 km east of YOSE. Fourteen active RAWS stations are currently located within 40 km of the boundaries of YOSE. The closest of these RAWS stations to YOSE are "Jerseydale" (2002-present), 12 km southwest of YOSE, and "Miami" (2004-present), 12 km south of YOSE. "Miami" has a large gap in its record from January to May of 2005; "Jerseydale," on the other hand, has a very complete data record. The longest records among the active RAWS stations come from "Mariposa" (29 km southwest of YOSE) and "Metcalf Gap" (13 km southwest of YOSE), both of which began taking observations in May 1990. "Mariposa" has a very complete data record except for one large gap from October 1993 to December 1994. "Metcalf Gap" has two gaps in its data record: one in July 1991 and the other in April and May of 1996. A SAO station is located at Mammoth Yosemite Airport, 36 km east of YOSE (Figure 4.1). This SAO station has been discussed previously. In addition to these stations, seven active SNOTEL stations have been identified within 40 km of YOSE. The longest records, which go back to October 1978, are furnished by three SNOTEL sites. "Lobdell Lake" is 33 km north of YOSE. "Sonora Pass" is 15 km north of YOSE. The third site, "Virginia Lakes Ridge," is 7 km northeast of YOSE. Two other longer records, going back to October 1980, are furnished by the sites "Leavitt Meadows" (9 km north of YOSE) and "Poison Flat" (35 km north of YOSE).

4.2.3. Sequoia and Kings Canyon National Parks

We identified 55 weather and climate stations within the boundaries of SEKI (Table 4.5). At least 26 of these stations are active presently. The CASTNet station "Ash Mountain," which has been active since 2005, is in southwestern SEKI (Figure 4.2). This station was located at Lookout Point along the East Fork of the Kaweah from 1997 through 2004. Nine active stations that provide data through the CDEC system are located inside SEKI. The longest CDEC records in SEKI come from the stations "Charlotte Lake" and "Crabtree Meadow," both of which started taking observations in October 1985. "Charlotte Lake" is in eastern SEKI, while "Crabtree Meadow" is on the eastern side of the Kern River valley in southeastern SEKI. The most recently installed CDEC station is "Farewell Gap," which has been taking observations only since October 2000. This station is near the southern boundary of SEKI.

Out of the 23 COOP stations we identified within SEKI, only three are active (Table 4.5). The longest record we identified was from the COOP station "Ash Mtn.," which is in southwestern SEKI and has been active since 1927. The record at this station is very complete after 1947. The same holds for the data record at "Grant Grove" (1940-present), which is near the western boundary of SEKI. The COOP station "Lodgepole" is located at the Lodgepole Visitor Center and has been active since 1951. The data record at this site is quite reliable. However, a possible station move occurred at this site in the autumn months of 1968. Park staff at SEKI have indicated that the COOP station "Giant Forest" (1921-1968) was moved to "Lodgepole" in 1968, so these two data records may overlap.

At least five GPMP sites and one NADP site are currently active inside SEKI (Table 4.5). The GPMP station "Ash Mountain (seki-as)," operational since 2000, is located in southwestern SEKI (Figure 4.2). Also located in southwestern SEKI is the GPMP station "Lower Kaweah," which has been operational since 1984. Collocated with this station is the NADP site "Sequoia NP-Giant Forest." This NADP site has been operational since 1980. Two weather stations operated by NPS were identified within SEKI. "ElkCreek" operated between 1983 and 2000 and was located in the foothills of southwestern SEKI. "MEWSS" is a NPS station that is located in the middle elevations of southwestern SEKI. This station took weather observations from 1984-2000.

Table 4.5. Weather and climate stations for SEKI. Stations inside SEKI and within 40 km of the park unit boundaries are included. Missing entries are indicated by "M".

Sequoia and Kings Canyon National Parks (SEKI)

Name	Lat.	Lon.	Elev. (m)	Network	Start	End	In Park?
Sequoia & Kings Cn. NP	36.488	-118.827	561	CARB	1984	2001	Yes
Sequoia NP – Lwr. Kaweah	36.562	-118.769	1900	CARB	1985	1998	Yes
Wolverton	36.601	-118.717	2130	CARB	1986	1999	Yes
Ash Mountain	36.489	-118.827	457	CASTNet	2005	Present	Yes
Sequoia/Kings Canyon NP	36.429	-118.763	1225	CASTNet	2/1/1997	12/31/2004	Yes
Bishop Pass	37.100	-118.557	3414	CDEC	1/1/1988	Present	Yes
Chagoopa Plateau	36.497	-118.442	3139	CDEC	10/1/1986	Present	Yes
Charlotte Lake	36.797	-118.422	3170	CDEC	10/1/1985	Present	Yes
Crabtree Meadow	36.563	-118.345	3261	CDEC	10/1/1985	Present	Yes
Farewell Gap	36.412	-118.583	2896	CDEC	10/1/2000	Present	Yes
Giant Forest (USACE)	36.562	-118.765	2027	CDEC	8/1/1988	Present	Yes
Mitchell Meadow	36.737	-118.712	3018	CDEC	8/1/1988	Present	Yes
State Lakes	36.927	-118.574	3139	CDEC	8/1/1988	Present	Yes
Upper Tyndall Creek	36.650	-118.397	3475	CDEC	8/1/1988	Present	Yes
Ash Mtn.	36.491	-118.825	521	COOP	1/1/1927	Present	Yes
Atwell	36.467	-118.667	1976	COOP	6/24/1948	10/1/1976	Yes
Bullfrog Lake	36.767	-118.400	3264	COOP	7/1/1948	7/31/1955	Yes
Cedar Grove	36.783	-118.667	1418	COOP	12/15/1940	5/23/1963	Yes
Chagoopa	36.500	-118.450	3154	COOP	7/1/1964	11/30/1972	Yes
Crabtree Meadow	36.567	-118.350	3264	COOP	7/1/1948	9/30/1976	Yes
Dusy Bench	37.100	-118.583	2888	COOP	7/1/1948	11/30/1972	Yes
East Vidette Meadow	36.733	-118.383	3172	COOP	4/28/1949	8/31/1964	Yes
Giant Forest	36.567	-118.767	1955	COOP	6/6/1921	11/8/1968	Yes
Giant Forest Radio	36.567	-118.767	2028	COOP	9/1/1965	9/30/1976	Yes
Granite Basin	36.867	-118.600	3050	COOP	7/1/1948	8/31/1964	Yes
Grant Grove	36.739	-118.963	2012	COOP	7/1/1940	Present	Yes
Hockett Meadows	36.367	-118.650	2593	COOP	8/1/1959	9/30/1976	Yes
Lewis Creek Kings Cn.	36.800	-118.683	1418	COOP	11/1/1945	7/25/1961	Yes
Lodgepole	36.604	-118.733	2053	COOP	2/1/1951	Present	Yes
Mineral King	36.433	-118.583	2434	COOP	8/1/1956	7/31/1969	Yes
Mitchell Meadow	36.733	-118.717	3020	COOP	8/1/1957	9/30/1976	Yes
Moraine Creek	36.717	-118.567	2696	COOP	8/1/1964	9/30/1974	Yes
Pear Lake	36.600	-118.667	2959	COOP	8/1/1956	9/30/1969	Yes
Rattlesnake Creek	36.983	-118.717	3020	COOP	6/1/1961	9/30/1976	Yes
State Lakes	36.933	-118.583	3142	COOP	7/1/1955	9/30/1976	Yes
Sugarloaf Meadow	36.717	-118.667	2196	COOP	7/1/1948	8/31/1957	Yes
Vidette Meadow	36.750	-118.417	2898	COOP	8/1/1964	9/30/1974	Yes
Ash Mountain (seki-am)	36.494	-118.829	610	GPMP	6/1/1982	10/1/1996	Yes
Ash Mountain (seki-as)	36.494	-118.829	610	GPMP	2000	Present	Yes
Lookout Point (seki-lp)	36.429	-118.763	1225	GPMP	1983	2005	Yes

Sequoia and Kings Canyon National Parks (SEKI)

Name	Lat.	Lon.	Elev. (m)	Network	Start	End	In Park?
Grant Grove	36.740	-118.961	2012	GPMP	12/1/1989	12/31/1995	Yes
Lower Kaweah	36.566	-118.777	1890	GPMP	6/1/1984	Present	Yes
Sequoia NP-Giant Forest	36.567	-118.777	1902	NADP	7/8/1980	Present	Yes
ElkCreek	36.513	-118.809	M	NPS	1/1/1983	12/31/2000	Yes
MEWSS	36.554	-118.752	M	NPS	1984	2000	Yes
Ash Mountain	36.491	-118.825	527	RAWS	12/1/2004	Present	Yes
Cedar Grove	36.788	-118.656	1439	RAWS	9/1/1999	Present	Yes
Milk Ranch	36.487	-118.780	1897	RAWS	8/1/1997	8/31/1999	Yes
Park Ridge	36.724	-118.943	2298	RAWS	7/1/1997	Present	Yes
Rattlesnake	36.407	-118.422	2621	RAWS	7/1/1992	Present	Yes
Sugarloaf	36.727	-118.675	2475	RAWS	7/1/1992	Present	Yes
Wolverton	36.445	-118.703	1597	RAWS	6/1/1996	Present	Yes
Emerald Lake	36.598	-118.674	2808	UCSB	8/1/1990	Present	Yes
Marble Fork	36.608	-118.685	2619	UCSB	8/1/1992	Present	Yes
M3	36.610	-118.647	3232	UCSB	3/1/1994	Present	Yes
Topaz Lake	36.625	-118.639	3221	UCSB	11/1/1995	Present	Yes
BAMI14	36.900	-119.310	520	BAMI	M	Present	No
Pinehurst	36.695	-119.019	1250	CARB	M	Present	No
Visalia	36.333	-119.291	97	CARB	M	Present	No
Big Meadows (DWR)	36.717	-118.842	2316	CDEC	10/1/1985	Present	No
Big Pine Creek	37.128	-118.475	2987	CDEC	9/1/1988	Present	No
Blackcap Basin	37.067	-118.770	3139	CDEC	10/1/1989	Present	No
Casa Vieja Meadows	36.200	-118.268	2530	CDEC	9/1/1987	Present	No
Cottonwood Lakes	36.483	-118.177	3094	CDEC	1/1/1986	Present	No
Huntington Lake (USBR)	37.228	-119.221	2134	CDEC	7/1/1998	Present	No
Kaiser Point	37.300	-119.100	2804	CDEC	9/1/1998	Present	No
Quaking Aspen	36.117	-118.540	2195	CDEC	10/1/1985	Present	No
Rock Creek Lakes	37.455	-118.743	3048	CDEC	1/1/1986	Present	No
Sawmill	37.162	-118.562	3109	CDEC	8/1/1988	Present	No
South Lake	37.176	-118.562	2926	CDEC	10/1/1985	Present	No
Tamarack Summit	37.165	-119.200	2301	CDEC	7/1/1998	Present	No
Tunnel Guard Station	36.367	-118.288	2713	CDEC	10/1/1985	Present	No
Upper Burnt Corral	37.183	-118.937	2957	CDEC	11/1/1986	Present	No
Volcanic Knob	37.388	-118.903	3063	CDEC	8/1/1989	Present	No
W. Woodchuck Mdw. Cal.	37.030	-118.918	2774	CDEC	10/1/1988	Present	No
Wet Meadow	36.348	-118.572	2728	CDEC	10/1/1988	Present	No
Bishop	37.358	-118.404	1271	CIMIS	2/1/1983	Present	No
Lindcove	36.357	-119.059	146	CIMIS	5/1/1989	Present	No
Orange Cove	36.721	-119.388	137	CIMIS	1/1/1999	Present	No
Owens Lake North	36.489	-117.919	1123	CIMIS	12/1/2002	Present	No
Owens Lake South	36.359	-117.946	1122	CIMIS	4/1/2003	Present	No
Porterville	36.081	-119.092	122	CIMIS	8/1/2000	Present	No

Sequoia and Kings Canyon National Parks (SEKI)

Name	Lat.	Lon.	Elev. (m)	Network	Start	End	In Park?
Visalia	36.301	-119.223	107	CIMIS	1/1/1983	Present	No
Badger	36.629	-119.012	933	COOP	7/1/1948	12/1/2006	No
Balch Pwr. House	36.909	-119.088	524	COOP	2/1/1950	Present	No
Barton Flat	36.817	-118.883	1147	COOP	7/1/1961	9/30/1972	No
Beartrap Meadow	36.683	-118.867	2074	COOP	8/1/1959	9/30/1976	No
Big Creek P.H. 1	37.206	-119.242	1487	COOP	6/1/1915	Present	No
Big Pine Creek	37.133	-118.483	3068	COOP	7/1/1948	9/30/1976	No
Bishop Arpt.	37.371	-118.358	1250	COOP	8/1/1930	Present	No
Bishop Ck. Intake 2	37.248	-118.581	2485	COOP	10/1/1959	12/27/2006	No
Bishop Creek	37.240	-118.599	2591	COOP	1/1/1931	Present	No
Bishop F.S.	37.368	-118.365	1252	COOP	11/21/1996	8/25/2005	No
Bishop Union Carbide	37.367	-118.717	2864	COOP	5/1/1957	5/6/1970	No
Camp Wishon	36.183	-118.667	1159	COOP	7/1/1948	11/30/1971	No
Cliff Camp	37.000	-119.000	1882	COOP	1/1/1931	12/31/1947	No
Cottonwood Creek	36.483	-118.183	3099	COOP	7/1/1948	9/30/1976	No
Doublebunk Meadow	35.950	-118.600	1891	COOP	8/1/1955	12/31/1972	No
Dunlap	36.750	-119.117	592	COOP	7/1/1937	1/31/1950	No
Dunlap Shingle Mill	36.717	-119.117	610	COOP	3/13/1948	8/25/1949	No
Dusy Bench	37.100	-118.583	2888	COOP	7/1/1948	11/30/1972	No
Eagle Creek	35.983	-118.650	2028	COOP	11/1/1964	9/30/1976	No
Exeter Fauver Ranch	36.350	-119.067	134	COOP	7/1/1948	9/1/1988	No
Horse Corral Meadow	36.750	-118.767	2342	COOP	7/1/1948	8/31/1959	No
Hossack	36.183	-118.617	2166	COOP	8/1/1959	9/30/1976	No
Huntington Lake	37.228	-119.221	2140	COOP	6/1/1915	Present	No
Independence	36.798	-118.204	1204	COOP	1/1/1893	Present	No
Independence Onion V	36.767	-118.333	2800	COOP	12/1/1948	2/25/1971	No
Johnsondale	35.967	-118.533	1427	COOP	11/1/1954	5/9/1979	No
Kern River Intake 3	35.950	-118.483	1113	COOP	10/1/1952	9/1/1966	No
Lake Sabrina	37.213	-118.614	2763	COOP	1/1/1925	12/27/2006	No
Lemon Cove	36.382	-119.026	156	COOP	1/1/1899	Present	No
Lindsay	36.203	-119.058	128	COOP	12/1/1913	Present	No
Lone Pine Cottnwd. P.H.	36.443	-118.043	1155	COOP	7/1/1948	Present	No
McKay Point	36.400	-119.050	137	COOP	10/1/1963	10/31/1964	No
Meadow Brook	37.100	-118.833	2959	COOP	7/1/1948	8/31/1951	No
Milo 5 NE	36.276	-118.768	945	COOP	1/1/1957	9/1/2006	No
Miramonte Conserv. Camp	36.663	-119.083	916	COOP	1/1/1957	Present	No
Monache Meadows	36.217	-118.167	2410	COOP	7/1/1948	9/30/1972	No
Mt. Givens	37.283	-119.083	2898	COOP	10/1/1963	4/1/1969	No
Mtn. Home	36.250	-118.717	1635	COOP	10/1/1962	9/30/1976	No
Orange Cove	36.617	-119.300	131	COOP	6/1/1931	5/1/1991	No
Peppermint Meadows	36.100	-118.500	1617	COOP	7/1/1948	8/31/1955	No
Piedra	36.800	-119.383	177	COOP	3/1/1912	11/1/1964	No

Sequoia and Kings Canyon National Parks (SEKI)

Name	Lat.	Lon.	Elev. (m)	Network	Start	End	In Park?
Pine Flat Dam	36.824	-119.336	186	COOP	11/1/1964	Present	No
Porterville	36.068	-119.020	120	COOP	6/1/1902	6/30/2004	No
Post Corral Meadow	37.117	-118.900	2507	COOP	9/1/1951	8/31/1959	No
Quaking Aspen	36.117	-118.533	2196	COOP	7/1/1955	8/31/1972	No
Quinn R.S.	36.333	-118.583	2532	COOP	7/1/1948	8/31/1959	No
Rock Creek	37.450	-118.733	2949	COOP	7/1/1948	9/30/1976	No
Rogers Camp	36.100	-118.633	1903	COOP	9/1/1964	9/30/1976	No
Rose Marie Meadow	37.317	-118.867	3050	COOP	10/1/1953	9/30/1976	No
Round Meadow	35.967	-118.350	2745	COOP	7/1/1948	8/31/1971	No
South Lake	37.168	-118.571	2920	COOP	12/1/1924	12/27/2006	No
Springville 3 ENE	36.150	-118.767	445	COOP	2/1/1951	10/31/1953	No
Springville 7 ENE	36.167	-118.700	753	COOP	10/1/1953	10/31/1974	No
Springville R.S.	36.142	-118.811	320	COOP	7/1/1948	9/1/2006	No
Springville Tule Hd.	36.193	-118.657	1241	COOP	1/1/1896	9/1/2006	No
Statum Meadow	36.933	-118.917	2532	COOP	7/1/1948	8/31/1959	No
Three Rivers 6 SE	36.368	-118.848	590	COOP	1/1/1957	Present	No
Three Rivers Edison P.H. 2	36.467	-118.883	290	COOP	8/1/1909	6/7/1971	No
Three Rivers Edison P.H. 1	36.465	-118.862	347	COOP	7/1/1948	Present	No
Trout Meadows	36.200	-118.417	1906	COOP	7/1/1948	7/31/1955	No
Tunnel R.S.	36.367	-118.283	2730	COOP	7/1/1948	9/30/1976	No
Vermilion Valley	37.367	-118.983	2294	COOP	12/1/1946	9/30/1976	No
Wet Meadow	36.350	-118.567	2730	COOP	8/1/1959	9/30/1976	No
Wishon Dam	37.007	-118.984	1996	COOP	11/1/1966	11/30/2005	No
Woodchuck Meadow	37.033	-118.900	2806	COOP	6/24/1955	10/7/1969	No
Worth Bridge	36.050	-118.933	159	COOP	2/1/1957	1/1/1965	No
CW0961 Visalia	36.313	-119.270	104	CWOP	M	Present	No
CW1000 Porterville	36.093	-119.062	105	CWOP	M	Present	No
CW4177 Three Rivers	36.478	-118.844	378	CWOP	M	Present	No
CW4849 Crowley Lake	37.564	-118.742	2105	CWOP	M	Present	No
CW5634 Camp Nelson	36.104	-118.524	2195	CWOP	M	Present	No
WA6YLB Exeter	36.290	-119.149	115	CWOP	M	Present	No
Independence	36.802	-118.196	1201	DRI	2/1/2004	Present	No
Independence 1SSW #03	36.786	-118.208	1274	DRI	1/1/2004	Present	No
Independence 2ESE #04	36.795	-118.166	1170	DRI	1/1/2004	Present	No
Independence 3S #09	36.766	-118.190	1238	DRI	1/1/2004	Present	No
Independence 3SE #10	36.773	-118.163	1179	DRI	1/1/2004	Present	No
Independence 3SSW #08	36.761	-118.229	1440	DRI	1/1/2004	Present	No
Independence 3SW #02	36.778	-118.243	1476	DRI	1/1/2004	Present	No
Independence 4E #05	36.801	-118.133	1145	DRI	1/1/2004	Present	No
Independence 4ESE #11	36.781	-118.128	1146	DRI	1/1/2004	Present	No
Independence 4SW #07	36.754	-118.254	1575	DRI	1/1/2004	Present	No
Independence 5ESE #12	36.785	-118.107	1137	DRI	1/1/2004	Present	No

Sequoia and Kings Canyon National Parks (SEKI)

Name	Lat.	Lon.	Elev. (m)	Network	Start	End	In Park?
Independence 5SSE #14	36.729	-118.171	1233	DRI	1/1/2004	Present	No
Independence 5WSW #01	36.768	-118.276	1736	DRI	1/1/2004	Present	No
Independence 6E #06	36.811	-118.091	1216	DRI	1/1/2004	Present	No
Independence 6S #13	36.719	-118.204	1440	DRI	1/1/2004	Present	No
Independence 6SE #15	36.741	-118.116	1136	DRI	1/1/2004	Present	No
Independence 7SE #16	36.740	-118.088	1136	DRI	1/1/2004	Present	No
Bishop	37.371	-118.366	1252	NADP	4/15/1980	6/22/1982	No
Blackrock	36.093	-118.260	2499	RAWS	7/1/1999	Present	No
Case Mountain	36.411	-118.809	1966	RAWS	5/1/2002	Present	No
Dinkey	37.066	-119.039	1728	RAWS	6/1/2000	Present	No
Fence Meadow	36.961	-119.175	1539	RAWS	6/1/1999	Present	No
Fish Slough	37.478	-118.408	1372	RAWS	4/1/1999	3/31/2005	No
High Sierra	37.315	-119.038	2256	RAWS	7/1/2001	Present	No
Johnsondale	35.972	-118.545	1433	RAWS	6/1/1998	Present	No
Milo	36.232	-118.871	610	RAWS	7/1/2001	Present	No
Mount Tom	37.376	-119.178	2749	RAWS	8/1/1999	7/31/2005	No
Oak Creek	36.843	-118.259	1480	RAWS	10/1/1994	Present	No
Oak Opening	36.175	-118.702	988	RAWS	2/1/1996	Present	No
Owens Valley	37.390	-118.551	1414	RAWS	9/1/1992	Present	No
Peppermint California	36.073	-118.541	2251	RAWS	12/1/2004	Present	No
Pinehurst	36.685	-119.000	1237	RAWS	4/1/2001	Present	No
Rock Creek	37.551	-118.667	2146	RAWS	6/1/1999	Present	No
Shadequarter	36.567	-118.956	1240	RAWS	5/1/1990	Present	No
Shaver	37.135	-119.255	1768	RAWS	4/1/1995	Present	No
Trimmer	36.911	-119.305	469	RAWS	6/1/1999	Present	No
Bishop Arpt.	37.371	-118.358	1250	SAO	8/1/1930	Present	No
Porterville AAF	36.033	-119.067	132	SAO	3/1/1945	10/31/1945	No
Bishop AAF	37.350	-118.400	1256	WBAN	1/1/1943	1/31/1944	No
Visalia	36.313	-119.270	102	WX4U	M	Present	No

The University of California, Santa Barbara (UCSB) operates four stations within SEKI (Table 4.5). These stations are located primarily in the upper Marble Fork of the Kaweah watershed.

Seven RAWS stations were identified within SEKI; six of these are active currently (Table 4.5), providing near-real-time weather data for SEKI. The most reliable data records come from the RAWS stations "Cedar Grove" (1999-present), in western SEKI (Figure 4.2), and "Wolverton" (1996-present), in southwestern SEKI. Both of these stations are free of data gaps lasting one month or longer. The Wolverton RAWS station is not to be confused with the CARB station also called "Wolverton" (see Table 4.5). This site was operated collaboratively by CARB, NOAA, and NPS and took observations near Lodgepole from 1986 to 1999. Two RAWS stations in SEKI are summer-only stations. These stations are "Rattlesnake" and "Sugarloaf," both of which began taking observations in July 1992. The RAWS station "Ash Mountain," in southwestern

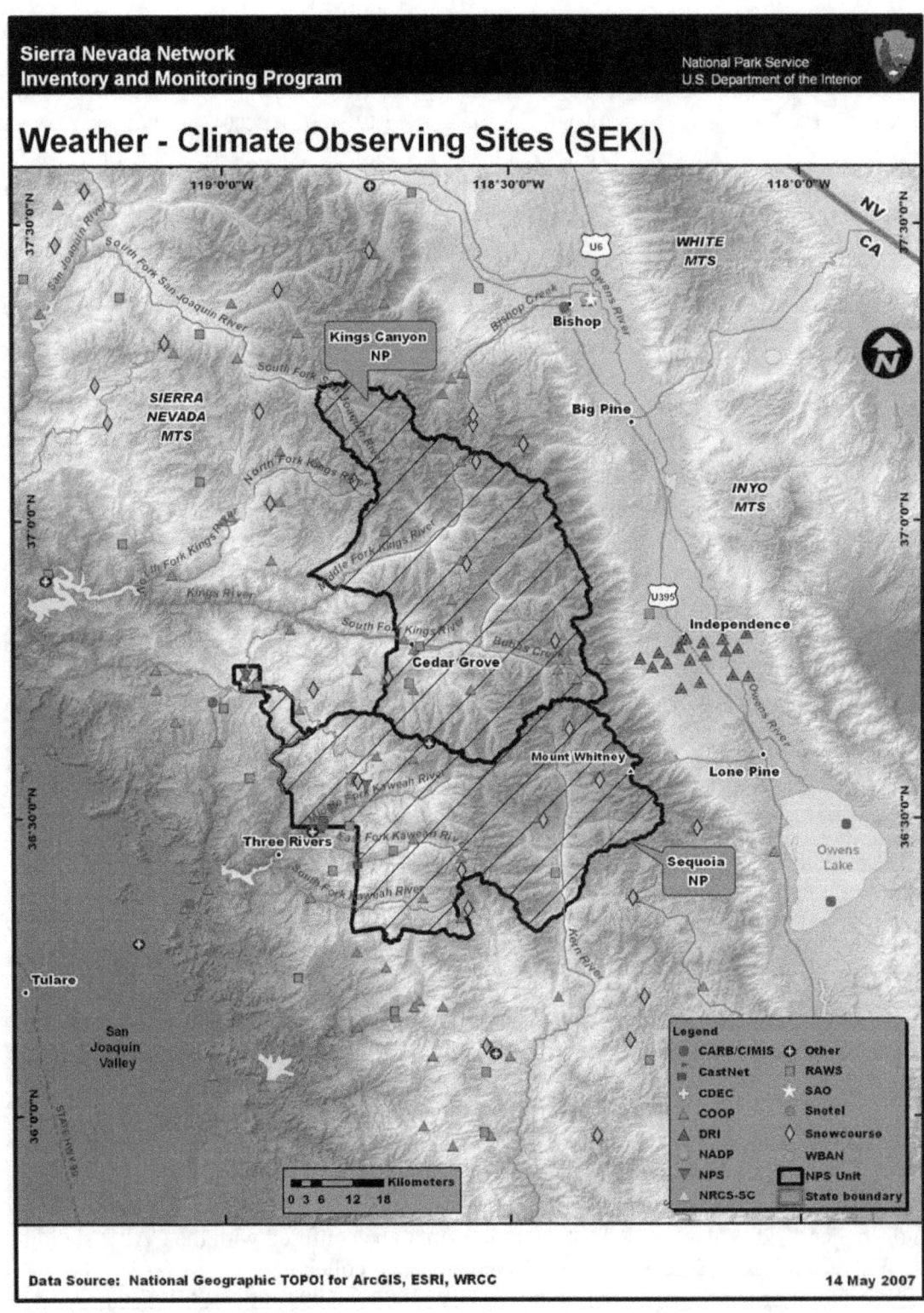

Figure 4.2. Station locations for SEKI.

SEKI, has been active since December 2004, yet had no data between January 2005 and February 2006. The RAWS station "Park Ridge" is in extreme western SEKI and has been active since July 1997. The data record at this site has been quite complete since May 2001.

One BAMI weather station was identified within 40 km of the boundaries of SEKI (Table 4.5). This station (BAMI14) is about 30 km west of SEKI, near Pine Flat Reservoir (Figure 4.2). Two CARB stations operate within 40 km of SEKI. "Pinehurst-NPS" is just west of SEKI, while "Visalia" is 40 km southwest of SEKI. Seventeen CDEC stations are active within 40 km of SEKI. The closest of these stations to SEKI is "Wet Meadow" (1988-present), located just 2 km south of SEKI. Seven active CIMIS stations are active within 40 km of SEKI. The closest CIMIS station to SEKI is "Lindcove" (1989-present), which is 21 km southwest of SEKI.

Out of the 66 COOP stations identified within 40 km of the boundaries of SEKI, only 13 are active (Table 4.5). The longest record we identified was from the COOP station "Independence," which is 14 km east of SEKI and has been active since 1893. The record at this station is very complete with a couple of exceptions. First, there were no weekend observations at "Independence" between 1948 and 1970. Second, a significant data gap occurred between March 1946 and June 1948. Another long-term record was identified at the COOP station "Lemon Cove," which is 17 km southwest of SEKI and has been active since 1899. The data record at this site has been quite reliable since 1948. Three COOP stations have data records going back to the 1910s. The COOP station "Big Creek P.H. 1" (1915-present) is 36 km northwest of SEKI. Unfortunately, this data record has been heavily compromised, with a large gap from the early 1960s to the late 1990s. The COOP station "Huntington Lake" (1915-present) is 34 km northwest of SEKI. The temperature record at this site is largely complete, with only scattered, small data gaps, but the precipitation record has a significant gap all through the 1960s and the early 1970s. The third record which goes back to the 1910s is at the COOP station "Lindsay," which is 28 km southwest of SEKI and has been active since 1913. The data record at this site has been quite reliable since 1948. Four other active COOP stations have data records going back to the 1930s and 1940s. "Bishop Arpt." is 33 km northeast of SEKI and has been active since 1930. This station's data record is quite reliable. A SAO station (Bishop Arpt.) is also located at this site and has a data record which is also quite reliable except for a data gap from January 2001 to November 2002. "Bishop Creek" (1931-present) is 8 km north of SEKI and has a data record that has been mostly unreliable until 2003. The COOP station "Lone Pine Cottonwood PH" is 18 km east of SEKI and has been active since 1948. The COOP station "Three Rivers Edison P.H. 1" is 2 km southwest of SEKI and has been active since 1948, although its data record has been unreliable since 1972. A couple other active COOP stations we identified have data records beginning in the 1950s and 1960s. Unfortunately, several COOP stations with long-term records appear to have ceased taking observations in recent years. These include "Lake Sabrina" (1925-2006), "Porterville" (1902-2004), "South Lake" (1925-2006), and "Springville Tule Hd." (1896-2006).

Several weather networks provide near-real-time data within 40 km of SEKI (Table 4.5). Six CWOP stations are located within 40 km of SEKI; most of these are located west of SEKI (Figure 4.2). The DRI network operates 17 weather stations associated with the Sierra Rotors Project (T-REX) near Independence, California, about 20 km east of SEKI. The T-REX project is designed to study mountain-wave induced rotors in Owens Valley, on the east side of the

Sierra Nevada. Eighteen RAWS stations were identified within 40 km of SEKI; 15 of these are active. The longest data record comes from the stations "Shadequarter" (1990-present), located only 5 km southwest of SEKI. This station had a data gap from October 1993 to December 1994. On the other side of SEKI, "Oak Creek" (1994-present) is only 9 km east of the park unit. This site had data gaps in January 2001 and in January and February of 2007.

5.0. Conclusions and Recommendations

We have based our findings on an examination of available climate records within SIEN units, discussions with NPS staff and other collaborators, and prior knowledge of the area. Here, we offer an evaluation and general comments pertaining to the status, prospects, and needs for climate-monitoring capabilities in SIEN.

5.1. Sierra Nevada Network

Despite the relatively large numbers of weather and climate stations we have identified within SEKI and YOSE (55 and 41 stations, respectively), many of these stations are located along primary roadways or near visitor centers and other high-traffic areas within the park units. Many of these stations are also no longer active; this is particularly true for COOP stations in these park units. To date, we have identified 49 active stations within network boundaries (one in DEPO, 26 in SEKI, and 22 in YOSE). This leads to a relatively small number of long-term climate records that are available for SIEN park units. Only six active stations have observation records of 50 years or longer. Existing active COOP stations that have long-term records will hopefully continue to operate for the foreseeable future, as these records are valuable for climate-monitoring efforts in SIEN, including the effects of climate change on SIEN park units.

In the more remote areas of both SEKI and YOSE, the primary sources of weather data come from stations that provide data through the CDEC system, primarily CSS sites. It is therefore beneficial for climate monitoring efforts in the SIEN that the NPS work closely with local agencies responsible for operating these CDEC stations to encourage the continued operation of these remote sites. Additional sites in more remote and high elevation areas would enhance climate monitoring in SIEN parks. Parks should evaluate the information that would be derived from enhancing climate monitoring and the trade-offs with environmental impact considerations and costs associated with remote monitoring. Several research groups are making valuable measurements of weather and climate elements within SIEN parks. These measurements will hopefully be encouraged to continue as well. Examples of such research efforts include the stations operated by the Scripps Institution of Oceanography, the University of Washington, and the University of California, Santa Barbara.

With many of the weather and climate stations within YOSE being located along the main roadways (e.g., Tioga Road) or in areas receiving higher visitor traffic, such as Yosemite Village, significant tracts of land within the park unit remain unsampled, primarily in northeastern and southeastern YOSE. We acknowledge that these areas are quite remote, as they are located in designated Wilderness with very difficult access. However, the overall understanding of the spatial characteristics of weather and climate patterns in YOSE would benefit greatly if weather and climate data could be obtained from these unsampled locations. One suitable strategy would be to install CSS stations in these areas. Many of the CSS sites currently in YOSE measure near-real-time temperature and precipitation and are located in remote locations, and therefore, would be suitable for the remote unsampled areas. See Section 5.2 for initial guidelines on installing new weather and climate stations.

With the exception of a few CDEC sites, few stations sample weather conditions in the higher elevations of SEKI. Like YOSE, the remoteness of eastern portions of SEKI and the Wilderness designation makes it difficult to install and maintain the stations that are needed to better sample the spatial characteristics of weather and climate within SEKI. Additional analyses could be conducted to evaluate the need for (and locations for) additional high-elevation sites. The RAWS station "Rattlesnake" is the only RAWS station in eastern SEKI but currently, it only takes observations during the summer. The NPS may want to consider expanding operations at this site in order to include fall, winter, and spring observations. Several long-term stations (COOP stations) in and near SEKI appear to have ceased taking measurements within the last couple of years. This is an unfortunate occurrence, as each of these records can provide valuable climate information for SEKI. For such stations that are inside SEKI, we recommend that the NPS consider re-activating these sites. For the recently-ended long-term climate stations outside of SEKI, we encourage the NPS to work with the local persons or agencies responsible for maintaining those long-term sites and encourage them to resume measurements at these valuable climate stations.

5.2. Spatial Variations in Mean Climate

With local variations over short horizontal and vertical distances, topography introduces considerable fine-scale structure to mean climate (temperature and precipitation) within the SIEN park units. Issues encountered in mapping mean climate are discussed in Appendix D and in Redmond et al. (2005).

For areas where new stations will be installed, if only a few new stations will be emplaced, the primary goal should be overall characterization of the main climate elements (temperature and precipitation and their joint relative, snow). This level of characterization generally requires that (a) stations should not be located in deep valley bottoms (cold air drainage pockets) or near excessively steep slopes and (b) stations should be distributed spatially in the major biomes of each park. If such stations already are present in the vicinity, then additional stations would be best used for two important and somewhat competing purposes: (a) add redundancy as backup for loss of data from current stations (or loss of the physical stations) or (b) provide added information on spatial heterogeneity in climate arising from topographic diversity.

5.3. Climate Change Detection

There is much interest in the adaptation of SIEN ecosystems in response to possible future climate change. In particular, there are concerns about snowpack trends in response to climate changes and the ability of plant and animal communities to adapt to climate change (Mutch et al. 2005). The SIEN region is strongly affected by ENSO cycles. Future climate changes could affect the frequency, intensity, and duration of ENSO events in the area, which would in turn impact SIEN ecosystems.

The desire for credible, accurate, complete, and long-term climate records—from any location—cannot be overemphasized. Thus, this consideration always should have a high priority. However, because of spatial diversity in climate, monitoring that fills knowledge gaps and provides information on long-term temporal variability in short-distance relationships also will be valuable. We cannot be sure that climate variability and climate change will affect all parts of a given park unit equally. In fact, it is appropriate to speculate that this is not the case, and spatial variations in temporal variability extend to small spatial scales, a consequence of diversity within SIEN in both topography and in land use patterns.

5.4. Aesthetics

This issue arises frequently enough to deserve comment. Standards for quality climate measurements require open exposures away from heat sources, buildings, pavement, close vegetation and tall trees, and human intrusion (thus away from property lines). By their nature, sites that meet these standards are usually quite visible. In many settings (such as heavily forested areas) these sites also are quite rare, making them precisely the same places that managers wish to protect from aesthetic intrusion. The most suitable and scientifically defensible sites frequently are rejected as candidate locations for weather and climate stations. Most weather and climate stations, therefore, tend to be "hidden" but many of these hidden locations have inferior exposures. Some measure of compromise is nearly always called for in siting weather and climate stations.

The public has vast interest and curiosity in weather and climate, and within the NPS I&M networks, such measurements consistently rate near or at the top of desired public information. There seem to be many possible opportunities for exploiting and embracing this widespread interest within the interpretive mission of the NPS. One way to do this would be to highlight rather than hide these stations and educate the public about the need for adequate siting. A number of weather displays we have encountered during visits have proven inadvertently to serve as counterexamples for how measurements should not be made.

5.5. Information Access

Access to information promotes its use, which in turn promotes attention to station care and maintenance, better data, and more use. An end-to-end view that extends from sensing to decision support is far preferable to isolated and disconnected activities and aids the support infrastructure that is ultimately so necessary for successful, long-term climate monitoring.

Decisions about improvements in monitoring capacity are facilitated greatly by the ability to examine available climate information. Various methods are being created at WRCC to improve access to that information. Web pages providing historic and ongoing climate data, and information from SIEN park units can be accessed at http://www.wrcc.dri.edu/nps. In the event that this URL changes, there still will be links from the main WRCC Web page entitled "Projects" under NPS.

The WRCC has been steadily developing software to summarize data from hourly sites. This has been occurring under the aegis of the RAWS program and a growing array of product generators ranging from daily and monthly data lists to wind roses and hourly frequency distributions. All park data are available to park personnel via an access code (needed only for data listings) that can be acquired by request. The WRCC RAWS Web page is located at http://www.wrcc.dri.edu/wraws or http://www.raws.dri.edu.

Web pages have been developed to provide access not only to historic and ongoing climate data and information from SIEN park units but also to climate-monitoring efforts for SIEN. These pages can be found through http://www.wrcc.dri.edu/nps.

Additional access to more standard climate information is accessible though the previously mentioned Web pages, as well as through http://www.wrcc.dri.edu/summary. These summaries are generally for COOP stations.

5.6. Summarized Conclusions and Recommendations

- Despite numerous weather and climate stations being identified in both SEKI and YOSE, most of these are located in more accessible areas and most are no longer active.
- Few long-term records exist inside SIEN park units. Climate monitoring efforts in SIEN will benefit by continuing the operation of those long-term climate stations identified in and near SIEN park units.
- Weather and climate conditions in remote, higher-elevation areas of SEKI and YOSE are not well-sampled. CDEC stations such as near-real-time California Cooperative Snow Survey sites provide main data source in these remote areas. Additional analyses could be conducted to evaluate the need for (and locations for) additional high-elevation sites.
- Various research groups monitor specific weather and climate elements in SIEN parks, including groups from Scripps Institution of Oceanography, the University of Washington, and the University of California, Santa Barbara.
- Eastern portions of SEKI have limited weather and climate station coverage, consisting mainly of CDEC sites. The seasonal RAWS station "Rattlesnake," in southeastern SEKI, could be expanded to year-round operation.

6.0 Literature Cited

American Association of State Climatologists. 1985. Heights and exposure standards for sensors on automated weather stations. The State Climatologist **9**.

Anderson, R. S. 1990. Holocene forest development and paleoclimates within the central Sierra Nevada, California. Journal of Ecology **78**:470-489.

Anderson, R. S. 1994. Paleohistory of a giant sequoia grove: The record from Log Meadow, Sequoia National Park. *In* P. S. Aune, editor. Proceedings of the Symposium on Giant Sequoias: Their place in the ecosystem and society. Vol. PSW-151.

Anderson, R. S., and S. J. Smith. 1991. Paleoecology within California's Sierra Nevada National Parks: An overview of the past and prospectus for the future. In: Proceedings of the Yosemite Centennial Symposium, El Portal, California.

Anderson, R. S., and S. J. Smith. 1994. Paleoclimatic interpretations of meadow sediment and pollen stratigraphies from California. Geology **22**:723-726.

Anderson, R. S., and S. J. Smith. 1997. Sedimentary record of fire in montane meadows, Sierra Nevada, California, USA: A preliminary assessment. Pages 313-327 *in* J. S. Clark, H. Cachier, J. G. Goldammer, and B. Stocks, editors. Sediment Records of Biomass Burning and Global Change. NATA ASI series, Springer-Verlag, Berlin.

Bonan, G. B. 2002. Ecological Climatology: Concepts and Applications. Cambridge University Press.

Bureau of Land Management. 1997. Remote Automatic Weather Station (RAWS) and Remote Environmental Monitoring Systems (REMS) standards. RAWS/REMS Support Facility, Boise, Idaho.

Cayan, D. R., M. D. Dettinger, H. F Diaz, and N. E. Graham. 1998. Decadal variability of precipitation over western North America. Journal of Climate **11**:3148-3166.

Cayan, D. R., S. A. Kammerdiener, M. D. Dettinger, J. M. Caprio, and D. H. Peterson. 2001. Changes in the onset of spring in the western United States. Bulletin of the American Meteorological Society **82**:399-415.

Chapin III, F. S., M. S. Torn, and M. Tateno. 1996. Principles of ecosystem sustainability. The American Naturalist **148**:1016-1037.

Daly, C., R. P. Neilson, and D. L. Phillips. 1994. A statistical-topographic model for mapping climatological precipitation over mountainous terrain. Journal of Applied Meteorology **33**:140-158.

Daly, C., W. P. Gibson, G. H. Taylor, G. L. Johnson, and P. Pasteris. 2002. A knowledge-based approach to the statistical mapping of climate. Climate Research **22**:99-113.

Dettinger, M. 2005a. Changes in Streamflow Timing in the Western United States in Recent Decades. Fact Sheet 2005-3018, US Geological Survey, Scripps Institution of Oceanography, La Jolla, California.

Dettinger, M. 2005b. Changes in Streamflow Timing in the Western United States in Recent Decades. National Streamflow Information Program, U.S. Geological Survey, Scripps Institution of Oceanography, La Jolla, California.

Dettinger, M. D., D. R. Cayan, M. Meyer, and A. E. Jeton. 2004. Simulated hydrologic responses to climate variations and change in the Merced, Carson, and American River basins, Sierra Nevada, California, 1900-2099. Climatic Change **62**:283-317.

Dettinger, M., K. Redmond, and D. Cayan. 2005. Winter Orographic-Precipitation Ratios in the Sierra Nevada - Large-Scale Atmospheric Circulations and Hydrologic Consequences. Journal of Hydrometeorology **5**:1102-1116.

Doggett, M., C. Daly, J. Smith, W. Gibson, G. Taylor, G. Johnson, and P. Pasteris. 2004. High-resolution 1971-2000 mean monthly temperature maps for the western United States. Fourteenth AMS Conf. on Applied Climatology, 84th AMS Annual Meeting. Seattle, Washington, American Meteorological Society, Boston, Massachusetts, January 2004, Paper 4.3, CD-ROM.

Dozier, J. 2004. The Sierra Nevada snowpack: Do the snow course data show historical trends? Eos Transactions AGU 85.

Environmental Protection Agency. 1987. On-site meteorological program guidance for regulatory modeling applications. EPA-450/4-87-013. Environmental Protection Agency, Office of Air Quality Planning and Standards, Research Triangle Park, North Carolina.

Finklin, A. I., and W. C. Fischer. 1990. Weather station handbook –an interagency guide for wildland managers. NFES No. 2140. National Wildfire Coordinating Group, Boise, Idaho.

Gibson, W. P., C. Daly, T. Kittel, D. Nychka, C. Johns, N. Rosenbloom, A. McNab, and G. Taylor. 2002. Development of a 103-year high-resolution climate data set for the conterminous United States. Thirteenth AMS Conf. on Applied Climatology. Portland, Oregon, American Meteorological Society, Boston, MA, May 2002:181-183.

Graumlich, L. J. 1993. A 1000-year record of temperature and precipitation in the Sierra Nevada. Quaternary Research **39**:249-255.

Hamlet, A. F., P. W. Mote, M. P. Clark, and D. P. Lettermaier. 2005. Effects of temperature and precipitation variability on snowpack trends in the western United States. Journal of Climate **18**:4545-4561.

Hayhoe, K., D. Cayan, C. B. Field, P. C. Frumhoff, E. P. Maurer, N. L. Miller, S. C. Moser, S. H. Schneider, K. N. Cahill, E. E. Cleland, and others. 2004. Emissions pathways, climate change, and impacts on California. National Academy of Sciences **101**:12422-12427.

Houghton, J. T., D. J. Ding, M. Griggs, M. Noguer, P. J. van der Linden, X. Dai, K. Maskell, and C. A. Johnson. 2001. Climate Change 2001: The Scientific Basis. Cambridge University Press, Cambridge, U.K.

Howat, I. M., and S. Tulaczyk. 2005. Climate sensitivity of spring snowpack in the Sierra Nevada. Journal of Geophysical Research **110**:10.1029/2005JF000356.

I&M. 2006. I&M Inventories home page. http://science.nature.nps.gov/im/inventory/index.cfm.

Jacobson, M. C., R. J. Charlson, H. Rodhe, and G. H. Orians. 2000. Earth System Science: From Biogeochemical Cycles to Global Change. Academic Press, San Diego.

Karl, T. R., V. E. Derr, D. R. Easterling, C. K. Folland, D. J. Hoffman, S. Levitus, N. Nicholls, D. E. Parker, and G. W. Withee. 1996. Critical issues for long-term climate monitoring. Pages 55-92 *in* T. R. Karl, editor. Long Term Climate Monitoring by the Global Climate Observing System, Kluwer Publishing.

Knowles, N., and D. R. Cayan. 2002. Potential effects of global warming on the Sacramento/San Joaquin watershed and the San Francisco estuary. Geophysical Research Letters **29**:1891.

Knowles, N., M. D. Dettinger, and D. R. Cayan. 2006. Trends in snowfall versus rainfall in the western United States. Journal of Climate **19**:4545-4559.

Lundquist, J. D., M. D. Dettinger, and D. R. Cayan. 2005. Snow-fed streamflow timing at different basin scales: Case study of the Tuolumne River above Hetch Hetchy, Yosemite, California. Water Resources Research **41**:10.1029/2004WR003933.

Mann, M. E., R. S. Bradley, and M. K. Hughes. 1998. Global-scale temperature patterns and climate forcing over the past six centuries. Nature **392**:779-787.

Mantua, N. J. 2000. The Pacific Decadal Oscillation and climate forecasting for North America. Online. (http://www.atmos.washington.edu/~mantua/REPORTS/PDO/PDO_cs.htm) Accessed 27 April 2004.

Mantua, N. J., and S. R. Hare. 2002. The Pacific decadal oscillation. Journal of Oceanography **58**:35-44.

Miller, C., and D. L. Urban. 1999. A model of surface fire, climate and forest pattern in the Sierra Nevada, California. Ecological Modeling **114**:113-135.

Mock, C. J. 1996. Climatic controls and spatial variations of precipitation in the Western United States. Journal of Climate **9**:1111-1125.

Mote, P. W., A. F. Hamlet, M. P. Clark, and D. P. Lettermaier. 2005. Declining mountain snowpack in western North America. Bulletin of the American Meteorological Society **86**:39-49.

Mutch, L., A. Heard, M. Rose, and S. Martens, editors. 2005. Vital Signs Monitoring Plan, Phase 2 Report, Sierra Nevada Network. Sierra Nevada Network, National Park Service.

National Assessment Synthesis Team. 2001. Climate Change Impacts on the United States: The Potential Consequences of Climate Variability and Change, Report for the U.S. Global Change Research Program. Cambridge University Press, Cambridge, UK.

National Research Council. 2001. A Climate Services Vision: First Steps Toward the Future. National Academies Press, Washington, D.C.

National Wildfire Coordinating Group. 2004. National fire danger rating system weather station standards. Report PMS 426.3. National Wildfire Coordinating Group, Boise, Idaho.

Neilson, R. P. 1987. Biotic regionalization and climatic controls in western North America. Vegetatio **70**:135-147.

Oakley, K. L., L. P. Thomas, and S. G. Fancy. 2003. Guidelines for long-term monitoring protocols. Wildlife Society Bulletin **31**:1000-1003.

Price, C., and D. Rind. 1991. Lightning activity in a greenhouse world. In: Proceedings of the 11th Conference of Fire and Forest Meteorology, Bethesda, Maryland.

Redmond, K. T., and R. W. Koch. 1991. Surface climate and streamflow variability in the western United States and their relationship to large-scale circulation indices. Water Resources Research **27**:2381-2399.

Redmond, K. T., D. B. Simeral, and G. D. McCurdy. 2005. Climate monitoring for southwest Alaska national parks: network design and site selection. Report 05-01. Western Regional Climate Center, Reno, Nevada.

Rodriguez-Iturbe, I. 2000. Ecohydrology: A hydrologic perspective of climate-soil-vegetation dynamics. Water Resources Research **36**:3-9.

Root, T. L., D. P. MacMynowski, M. D. Mastrandrea, and S. H. Schneider. 2005. Human-modified temperatures induce species changes: Joint attribution. National Academy of Sciences **102**:7465-7469.

Schlesinger, W. H. 1997. Biogeochemistry: An Analysis of Global Change. Academic Press, San Diego.

Snyder, M. A., J. L. Bell, L. C. Sloan, P. B. Duffy, and B. Govindasamy. 2002. Climate responses to a doubling of atmospheric carbon dioxide for a climatically vulnerable region. Geophysical Research Letters **29**:10.1029/2001GL014431.

Stephenson, N. L. 1988. Climatic control of vegetation distribution: The role of the water balance with examples from North America and Sequoia National Park, California. Cornell University, Ithaca, New York.

Stewart, I. T., D. R. Cayan, and M. D. Dettinger. 2004. Changes in snowmelt runoff timing in western North America under a 'business as usual' climate change scenario. Climatic Change **62**:217-232.

Stewart, I. T., D. R. Cayan, and M. D. Dettinger. 2005. Changes toward earlier streamflow timing across western North America. Journal of Climate **18**:1136-1155.

Tanner, B. D. 1990. Automated weather stations. Remote Sensing Reviews **5**:73-98.

Torn, M. S., and J. S. Fried. 1992. Predicting the impacts of global warming on wildland fire. Climatic Change **21**:257-274.

Wallace, J. M., and D. S. Gutzler. 1981. Teleconnections in the geopotential height field during the Northern Hemisphere winter. Monthly Weather Review **109**:784-812.

World Meteorological Organization. 1983. Guide to meteorological instruments and methods of observation, No. 8, 5th edition, World Meteorological Organization, Geneva, Switzerland.

World Meteorological Organization. 2005. Organization and planning of intercomparisons of rainfall intensity gauges. World Meteorological Organization, Geneva, Switzerland.

Appendix A. Glossary

Climate—Complete and entire ensemble of statistical descriptors of temporal and spatial properties comprising the behavior of the atmosphere. These descriptors include means, variances, frequency distributions, autocorrelations, spatial correlations and other patterns of association, temporal lags, and element-to-element relationships. The descriptors have a physical basis in flows and reservoirs of energy and mass. Climate and weather phenomena shade gradually into each other and are ultimately inseparable.

Climate Element—(same as Weather Element) Attribute or property of the state of the atmosphere that is measured, estimated, or derived. Examples of climate elements include temperature, wind speed, wind direction, precipitation amount, precipitation type, relative humidity, dewpoint, solar radiation, snow depth, soil temperature at a given depth, etc. A derived element is a function of other elements (like degree days or number of days with rain) and is not measured directly with a sensor. The terms "parameter" or "variable" are not used to describe elements.

Climate Network—Group of climate stations having a common purpose; the group is often owned and maintained by a single organization.

Climate Station—Station where data are collected to track atmospheric conditions over the long-term. Often, this station operates to additional standards to verify long-term consistency. For these stations, the detailed circumstances surrounding a set of measurements (siting and exposure, instrument changes, etc.) are important.

Data—Measurements specifying the state of the physical environment. Does not include metadata.

Data Inventory—Information about overall data properties for each station within a weather or climate network. A data inventory may include start/stop dates, percentages of available data, breakdowns by climate element, counts of actual data values, counts or fractions of data types, etc. These properties must be determined by actually reading the data and thus require the data to be available, accessible, and in a readable format.

NPS I&M Network—A set of NPS park units grouped by a common theme, typically by natural resource and/or geographic region.

Metadata—Information necessary to interpret environmental data properly, organized as a history or series of snapshots—data about data. Examples include details of measurement processes, station circumstances and exposures, assumptions about the site, network purpose and background, types of observations and sensors, pre-treatment of data, access information, maintenance history and protocols, observational methods, archive locations, owner, and station start/end period.

Quality Assurance—Planned and systematic set of activities to provide adequate confidence that products and services are resulting in credible and correct information. Includes quality control.

Quality Control—Evaluation, assessment, and improvement of imperfect data by utilizing other imperfect data.

Station Inventory—Information about a set of stations obtained from metadata that accompany the network or networks. A station inventory can be compiled from direct and indirect reports prepared by others.

Weather—Instantaneous state of the atmosphere at any given time, mainly with respect to its effects on biological activities. As distinguished from climate, weather consists of the short-term (minutes to days) variations in the atmosphere. Popularly, weather is thought of in terms of temperature, precipitation, humidity, wind, sky condition, visibility, and cloud conditions.

Weather Element (same as Climate Element)—Attribute or property of the state of the atmosphere that is measured, estimated, or derived. Examples of weather elements include temperature, wind speed, wind direction, precipitation amount, precipitation type, relative humidity, dewpoint, solar radiation, snow depth, soil temperature at a given depth, etc. A derived weather element is a function of other elements (like degree days or number of days with rain) and is not measured directly. The terms "parameter" and "variable" are not used to describe weather elements.

Weather Network—Group of weather stations usually owned and maintained by a particular organization and usually for a specific purpose.

Weather Station—Station where collected data are intended for near-real-time use with less need for reference to long-term conditions. In many cases, the detailed circumstances of a set of measurements (siting and exposure, instrument changes, etc.) from weather stations are not as important as for climate stations.

Appendix B. Climate-monitoring principles

Since the late 1990s, frequent references have been made to a set of climate-monitoring principles enunciated in 1996 by Tom Karl, director of the NOAA NCDC in Asheville, North Carolina. These monitoring principles also have been referred to informally as the "Ten Commandments of Climate Monitoring." Both versions are given here. In addition, these principles have been adopted by the Global Climate Observing System (GCOS 2004).

(Compiled by Kelly Redmond, Western Regional Climate Center, Desert Research Institute, August 2000.)

B.1. Full Version (Karl et al. 1996)

B.1.1. Effects on climate records of instrument changes, observing practices, observation locations, sampling rates, etc., must be known before such changes are implemented. This can be ascertained through a period where overlapping measurements from old and new observing systems are collected or sometimes by comparing the old and new observing systems with a reference standard. Site stability for in situ measurements, both in terms of physical location and changes in the nearby environment, also should be a key criterion in site selection. Thus, many synoptic network stations, which are primarily used in weather forecasting but also provide valuable climate data, and dedicated climate stations intended to be operational for extended periods must be subject to this policy.

B.1.2. Processing algorithms and changes in these algorithms must be well documented. Documentation should be carried with the data throughout the data-archiving process.

B.1.3. Knowledge of instrument, station, and/or platform history is essential for interpreting and using the data. Changes in instrument sampling time, local environmental conditions for in situ measurements, and other factors pertinent to interpreting the observations and measurements should be recorded as a mandatory part in the observing routine and be archived with the original data.

B.1.4. In situ and other observations with a long, uninterrupted record should be maintained. Every effort should be applied to protect the data sets that have provided long-term, homogeneous observations. "Long-term" for space-based measurements is measured in decades, but for more conventional measurements, "long-term" may be a century or more. Each element in the observational system should develop a list of prioritized sites or observations based on their contribution to long-term climate monitoring.

B.1.5. Calibration, validation, and maintenance facilities are critical requirements for long-term climatic data sets. Homogeneity in the climate record must be assessed routinely, and corrective action must become part of the archived record.

B.1.6. Where feasible, some level of "low-technology" backup to "high-technology" observing systems should be developed to safeguard against unexpected operational failures.

B.1.7. Regions having insufficient data, variables and regions sensitive to change, and key measurements lacking adequate spatial and temporal resolution should be given the highest priority in designing and implementing new climate-observing systems.

B.1.8. Network designers and instrument engineers must receive long-term climate requirements at the outset of the network design process. This is particularly important because most observing systems have been designed for purposes other than long-term climate monitoring. Instruments must possess adequate accuracy with biases small enough to document climate variations and changes.

B.1.9. Much of the development of new observational capabilities and the evidence supporting the value of these observations stem from research-oriented needs or programs. A lack of stable, long-term commitment to these observations and lack of a clear transition plan from research to operations are two frequent limitations in the development of adequate, long-term monitoring capabilities. Difficulties in securing a long-term commitment must be overcome in order to improve the climate-observing system in a timely manner with minimal interruptions.

B.1.10. Data management systems that facilitate access, use, and interpretation are essential. Freedom of access, low cost, mechanisms that facilitate use (directories, catalogs, browse capabilities, availability of metadata on station histories, algorithm accessibility and documentation, etc.) and quality control should guide data management. International cooperation is critical for successful management of data used to monitor long-term climate change and variability.

B.2. Abbreviated version, "Ten Commandments of Climate Monitoring"

B.2.1. Assess the impact of new climate-observing systems or changes to existing systems before they are implemented.

"Thou shalt properly manage network change." (assess effects of proposed changes)

B.2.2. Require a suitable period where measurement from new and old climate-observing systems will overlap.

"Thou shalt conduct parallel testing." (compare old and replacement systems)

B.2.3. Treat calibration, validation, algorithm-change, and data-homogeneity assessments with the same care as the data.

"Thou shalt collect metadata." (fully document system and operating procedures)

B.2.4. Verify capability for routinely assessing the quality and homogeneity of the data including high-resolution data for extreme events.

"Thou shalt assure data quality and continuity." (assess as part of routine operating procedures)

B.2.5. Integrate assessments like those conducted by the International Panel on Climate Change into global climate-observing priorities.

"Thou shalt anticipate the use of data." (integrated environmental assessment; component in operational plan for system)

B.2.6. Maintain long-term weather and climate stations.

"Thou shalt worship historic significance." (maintain homogeneous data sets from long–term, climate-observing systems)

B.2.7. Place high priority on increasing observations in regions lacking sufficient data and in regions sensitive to change and variability.

"Thou shalt acquire complementary data." (new sites to fill observational gaps)

B.2.8. Provide network operators, designers, and instrument engineers with long-term requirements at the outset of the design and implementation phases for new systems.

"Thou shalt specify requirements for climate observation systems." (application and usage of observational data)

B.2.9. Carefully consider the transition from research-observing system to long-term operation.

"Thou shalt have continuity of purpose." (stable long-term commitments)

B.2.10. Focus on data-management systems that facilitate access, use, and interpretation of weather data and metadata.

"Thou shalt provide access to data and metadata." (readily available weather and climate information)

B.3. Literature Cited

Karl, T. R., V. E. Derr, D. R. Easterling, C. K. Folland, D. J. Hoffman, S. Levitus, N. Nicholls, D. E. Parker, and G. W. Withee. 1996. Critical Issues for Long-Term Climate Monitoring. Pages 55-92 *in* T. R. Karl, editor. Long Term Climate Monitoring by the Global Climate Observing System, Kluwer Publishing.

Global Climate Observing System. 2004. Implementation Plan for the Global Observing System for Climate in Support of the UNFCCC. GCOS-92, WMO/TD No. 1219, World Meteorological Organization, Geneva, Switzerland.

Appendix C. Factors in operating a weather/ climate network

C.1. Climate versus Weather

- Climate measurements require *consistency through time.*

C.2. Network Purpose

- Anticipated or desired lifetime.
- Breadth of network mission (commitment by needed constituency).
- Dedicated constituency—no network survives without a dedicated constituency.

C.3. Site Identification and Selection

- Spanning gradients in climate or biomes with transects.
- Issues regarding representative spatial scale—site uniformity versus site clustering.
- Alignment with and contribution to network mission.
- Exposure—ability to measure representative quantities.
- Logistics—ability to service station (Always or only in favorable weather?).
- Site redundancy (positive for quality control, negative for extra resources).
- Power—is AC needed?
- Site security—is protection from vandalism needed?
- Permitting often a major impediment and usually underestimated.

C.4. Station Hardware

- Survival—weather is the main cause of lost weather/climate data.
- Robustness of sensors—ability to measure and record in any condition.
- Quality—distrusted records are worthless and a waste of time and money.
  - High quality—will cost up front but pays off later.
  - Low quality—may provide a lower start-up cost but will cost more later (low cost can be expensive).
- Redundancy—backup if sensors malfunction.
- Ice and snow—measurements are much more difficult than rain measurements.
- Severe environments (expense is about two–three times greater than for stations in more benign settings).

C.5. Communications

- Reliability—live data have a much larger constituency.
- One-way or two-way.
  - Retrieval of missed transmissions.
  - Ability to reprogram data logger remotely.
  - Remote troubleshooting abilities.
  - Continuing versus one-time costs.
- Back-up procedures to prevent data loss during communication outages.
- Live communications increase problems but also increase value.

C.6. Maintenance

- Main reason why networks fail (and most networks do eventually fail!).
- Key issue with nearly every network.
- Who will perform maintenance?
- Degree of commitment and motivation to contribute.
- Periodic? On-demand as needed? Preventive?
- Equipment change-out schedules and upgrades for sensors and software.
- Automated stations require skilled and experienced labor.
- Calibration—sensors often drift (climate).
- Site maintenance essential (constant vegetation, surface conditions, nearby influences).
- Typical automated station will cost about $2K per year to maintain.
- Documentation—photos, notes, visits, changes, essential for posterity.
- Planning for equipment life cycle and technological advances.

C.7. Maintaining Programmatic Continuity and Corporate Knowledge

- Long-term vision and commitment needed.
- Institutionalizing versus personalizing—developing appropriate dependencies.

C.8. Data Flow

- Centralized ingest?
- Centralized access to data and data products?
- Local version available?
- Contract out work or do it yourself?
- Quality control of data.
- Archival.
- Metadata—historic information, not a snapshot. Every station should collect metadata.
- Post-collection processing, multiple data-ingestion paths.

C.9. Products

- Most basic product consists of the data values.
- Summaries.
- Write own applications or leverage existing mechanisms?

C.10. Funding

- Prototype approaches as proof of concept.
- Linking and leveraging essential.
- Constituencies—every network needs a constituency.
- Bridging to practical and operational communities? Live data needed.
- Bridging to counterpart research efforts and initiatives—funding source.
- Creativity, resourcefulness, and persistence usually are essential to success.

C.11. Final Comments

- Deployment is by far the easiest part in operating a network.
- Maintenance is the main issue.
- Best analogy: Operating a network is like raising a child; it requires constant attention.

Source: Western Regional Climate Center (WRCC)

Appendix D. General design considerations for weather/ climate-monitoring programs

The process for designing a climate-monitoring program benefits from anticipating design and protocol issues discussed here. Much of this material is been excerpted from a report addressing the Channel Islands National Park (Redmond and McCurdy 2005), where an example is found illustrating how these factors can be applied to a specific setting. Many national park units possess some climate or meteorology feature that sets them apart from more familiar or "standard" settings.

D.1. Introduction
There are several criteria that must be used in deciding to deploy new stations and where these new stations should be sited.
- Where are existing stations located?
- Where have data been gathered in the past (discontinued locations)?
- Where would a new station fill a knowledge gap about basic, long-term climatic averages for an area of interest?
- Where would a new station fill a knowledge gap about how climate behaves over time?
- As a special case for behavior over time, what locations might be expected to show a more sensitive response to climate change?
- How do answers to the preceding questions depend on the climate element? Are answers the same for precipitation, temperature, wind, snowfall, humidity, etc.?
- What role should manual measurements play? How should manual measurements interface with automated measurements?
- Are there special technical or management issues, either present or anticipated in the next 5–15 years, requiring added climate information?
- What unique information is provided in addition to information from existing sites? "Redundancy is bad."
- What nearby information is available to estimate missing observations because observing systems always experience gaps and lose data? "Redundancy is good."
- How would logistics and maintenance affect these decisions?

In relation to the preceding questions, there are several topics that should be considered. The following topics are not listed in a particular order.

D.1.1. Network Purpose
Humans seem to have an almost reflexive need to measure temperature and precipitation, along with other climate elements. These reasons span a broad range from utilitarian to curiosity-driven. Although there are well-known recurrent patterns of need and data use, new uses are always appearing. The number of uses ranges in the thousands. Attempts have been made to categorize such uses (NRC 1998; NRC 2001). Because climate measurements are accumulated over a long time, they should be treated as multi-purpose and should be undertaken in a manner that serves the widest possible applications. Some applications remain constant, while others rise and fall in importance. An insistent issue today may subside, while the next pressing issue of tomorrow barely may be anticipated. The notion that humans might affect the climate of the

entire Earth was nearly unimaginable when the national USDA (later NOAA) cooperative weather network began in the late 1800s. Abundant experience has shown, however, that there always will be a demand for a history record of climate measurements and their properties. Experience also shows that there is an expectation that climate measurements will be taken and made available to the general public.

An exhaustive list of uses for data would fill many pages and still be incomplete. In broad terms, however, there are needs to document environmental conditions that disrupt or otherwise affect park operations (e.g., storms and droughts). Design and construction standards are determined by climatological event frequencies that exceed certain thresholds. Climate is a determinant that sometimes attracts and sometimes discourages visitors. Climate may play a large part in the park experience (e.g., Death Valley and heat are nearly synonymous). Some park units are large enough to encompass spatial or elevation diversity in climate and the sequence of events can vary considerably inside or close to park boundaries. That is, temporal trends and statistics may not be the same everywhere, and this spatial structure should be sampled. The granularity of this structure depends on the presence of topography or large climate gradients or both, such as that found along the U.S. West Coast in summer with the rapid transition from the marine layer to the hot interior.

Plant and animal communities and entire ecosystems react to every nuance in the physical environment. No aspect of weather and climate goes undetected in the natural world. Wilson (1998) proposed "an informal rule of biological evolution" that applies here: "If an organic sensor can be imagined that is capable of detecting any particular environmental signal, a species exists somewhere that possesses this sensor." Every weather and climate event, whether dull or extraordinary to humans, matters to some organism. Dramatic events and creeping incremental change both have consequences to living systems. Extreme events or disturbances can "reset the clock" or "shake up the system" and lead to reverberations that last for years to centuries or longer. Slow change can carry complex nonlinear systems (e.g., any living assemblage) into states where chaotic transitions and new behavior occur. These changes are seldom predictable, typically are observed after the fact, and understood only in retrospect. Climate changes may not be exciting, but as a well-known atmospheric scientist, Mike Wallace, from the University of Washington once noted, "subtle does not mean unimportant."

Thus, individuals who observe the climate should be able to record observations accurately and depict both rapid and slow changes. In particular, an array of artificial influences easily can confound detection of slow changes. The record as provided can contain both real climate variability (that took place in the atmosphere) and fake climate variability (that arose directly from the way atmospheric changes were observed and recorded). As an example, trees growing near a climate station with an excellent anemometer will make it appear that the wind gradually slowed down over many years. Great care must be taken to protect against sources of fake climate variability on the longer-time scales of years to decades. Processes leading to the observed climate are not stationary; rather these processes draw from probability distributions that vary with time. For this reason, climatic time series do not exhibit statistical stationarity. The implications are manifold. There are no true climatic "normals" to which climate inevitably must return. Rather, there are broad ranges of climatic conditions. Climate does not demonstrate exact repetition but instead continual fluctuation and sometimes approximate repetition. In addition, there is always new behavior waiting to occur. Consequently, the business of climate monitoring is never finished, and there is no point where we can state confidently that "enough" is known.

D.1.2. Robustness

The most frequent cause for loss of weather data is the weather itself, the very thing we wish to record. The design of climate and weather observing programs should consider the meteorological equivalent of "peaking power" employed by utilities. Because environmental disturbances have significant effects on ecologic systems, sensors, data loggers, and communications networks should be able to function during the most severe conditions that realistically can be anticipated over the next 50–100 years. Systems designed in this manner are less likely to fail under more ordinary conditions, as well as more likely to transmit continuous, quality data for both tranquil and active periods.

D.1.3. Weather versus Climate

For "weather" measurements, pertaining to what is approximately happening here and now, small moves and changes in exposure are not as critical. For "climate" measurements, where values from different points in time are compared, siting and exposure are critical factors, and it is vitally important that the observing circumstances remain essentially unchanged over the duration of the station record.

Station moves can affect different elements to differing degrees. Even small moves of several meters, especially vertically, can affect temperature records. Hills and knolls act differently from the bottoms of small swales, pockets, or drainage channels (Whiteman 2000; Geiger et al. 2003). Precipitation is probably less subject to change with moves of 50–100 m than other elements (that is, precipitation has less intrinsic variation in small spaces) except if wind flow over the gauge is affected.

D.1.4. Physical Setting

Siting and exposure, and their continuity and consistency through time, significantly influence the climate records produced by a station. These two terms have overlapping connotations. We use the term "siting" in a more general sense, reserving the term "exposure" generally for the particular circumstances affecting the ability of an instrument to record measurements that are representative of the desired spatial or temporal scale.

D.1.5. Measurement Intervals

Climatic processes occur continuously in time, but our measurement systems usually record in discrete chunks of time: for example, seconds, hours, or days. These measurements often are referred to as "systematic" measurements. Interval averages may hide active or interesting periods of highly intense activity. Alternatively, some systems record "events" when a certain threshold of activity is exceeded (examples: another millimeter of precipitation has fallen, another kilometer of wind has moved past, the temperature has changed by a degree, a gust higher than 9.9 m/s has been measured). When this occurs, measurements from all sensors are reported. These measurements are known as "breakpoint" data. In relatively unchanging conditions (long calm periods or rainless weeks, for example), event recorders should send a signal that they are still "alive and well." If systematic recorders are programmed to note and periodically report the highest, lowest, and mean value within each time interval, the likelihood is reduced that interesting behavior will be glossed over or lost. With the capacity of modern data loggers, it is recommended to record and report extremes within the basic time increment (e.g., hourly or 10 minutes). This approach also assists quality-control procedures.

There is usually a trade-off between data volume and time increment, and most automated systems now are set to record approximately hourly. A number of field stations maintained by WRCC are programmed to record in 5- or 10-minute increments, which readily serve to construct an hourly value. However, this approach produces 6–12 times as much data as hourly data. These systems typically do not record details of events at sub-interval time scales, but they easily can record peak values, or counts of threshold exceedance, within the time intervals.

Thus, for each time interval at an automated station, we recommend that several kinds of information—mean or sum, extreme maximum and minimum, and sometimes standard deviation—be recorded. These measurements are useful for quality control and other purposes. Modern data loggers and office computers have quite high capacity. Diagnostic information indicating the state of solar chargers or battery voltages and their extremes is of great value. This topic will be discussed in greater detail in a succeeding section.

Automation also has made possible adaptive or intelligent monitoring techniques where systems vary the recording rate based on detection of the behavior of interest by the software. Sub-interval behavior of interest can be masked on occasion (e.g., a 5-minute extreme downpour with high-erosive capability hidden by an innocuous hourly total). Most users prefer measurements that are systematic in time because they are much easier to summarize and manipulate.

For breakpoint data produced by event reporters, there also is a need to send periodically a signal that the station is still functioning, even though there is nothing more to report. "No report" does not necessarily mean "no data," and it is important to distinguish between the actual observation that was recorded and the content of that observation (e.g., an observation of "0.00" is not the same as "no observation").

D.1.6. Mixed Time Scales
There are times when we may wish to combine information from radically different scales. For example, over the past 100 years we may want to know how the frequency of 5-minute precipitation peaks has varied or how the frequency of peak 1-second wind gusts have varied. We may also want to know over this time if nearby vegetation gradually has grown up to increasingly block the wind or to slowly improve precipitation catch. Answers to these questions require knowledge over a wide range of time scales.

D.1.7. Elements
For manual measurements, the typical elements recorded included temperature extremes, precipitation, and snowfall/snow depth. Automated measurements typically include temperature, precipitation, humidity, wind speed and direction, and solar radiation. An exception to this exists in very windy locations where precipitation is difficult to measure accurately. Automated measurements of snow are improving, but manual measurements are still preferable, as long as shielding is present. Automated measurement of frozen precipitation presents numerous challenges that have not been resolved fully, and the best gauges are quite expensive ($3–8K).

Soil temperatures also are included sometimes. Soil moisture is extremely useful, but measurements are not made at many sites. In addition, care must be taken in the installation and maintenance of instruments used in measuring soil moisture. Soil properties vary tremendously in short distances as well, and it is often very difficult ("impossible") to accurately document these variations (without digging up all the soil!). In cooler climates, ultrasonic sensors that detect snow depth are becoming commonplace.

D.1.8. Wind Standards
Wind varies the most in the shortest distance, since it always decreases to zero near the ground and increases rapidly (approximately logarithmically) with height near the ground. Changes in anemometer height obviously will affect distribution of wind speed as will changes in vegetation, obstructions such as buildings, etc. A site that has a 3-m (10-ft) mast clearly will be less windy than a site that has a 6-m (20-ft) or 10-m (33-ft) mast. Historically, many U.S. airports (FAA and NWS) and most current RAWS sites have used a standard 6-m (20-ft) mast for wind measurements. Some NPS RAWS sites utilize shorter masts. Over the last decade, as Automated Surface Observing Systems (ASOSs, mostly NWS) and Automated Weather Observing Systems (AWOSs, mostly FAA) have been deployed at most airports, wind masts have been raised to 8 or 10 m (26 or 33 ft), depending on airplane clearance. The World Meteorological Organization recommends 10 m as the height for wind measurements (WMO 1983; 2005), and more groups are migrating slowly to this standard. The American Association of State Climatologists (AASC 1985) have recommended that wind be measured at 3 m, a standard geared more for agricultural applications than for general purpose uses where higher levels usually are preferred. Different anemometers have different starting thresholds; therefore, areas that frequently experience very light winds may not produce wind measurements thus affecting long-term mean estimates of wind speed. For both sustained winds (averages over a short interval of 2–60 minutes) and especially for gusts, the duration of the sampling interval makes a considerable difference. For the same wind history, 1–second gusts are higher than gusts averaging 3 seconds, which in turn are greater than 5-second averages, so that the same sequence would be described with different numbers (all three systems and more are in use). Changes in the averaging procedure, or in height or exposure, can lead to "false" or "fake" climate change with no change in actual climate. Changes in any of these should be noted in the metadata.

D.1.9. Wind Nomenclature
Wind is a vector quantity having a direction and a speed. Directions can be two- or three-dimensional; they will be three-dimensional if the vertical component is important. In all common uses, winds always are denoted by the direction they blow *from* (north wind or southerly breeze). This convention exists because wind often brings weather, and thus our attention is focused upstream. However, this approach contrasts with the way ocean currents are viewed. Ocean currents usually are denoted by the direction they are moving *towards* (eastward current moves from west to east). In specialized applications (such as in atmospheric modeling), wind velocity vectors point in the direction that the wind is blowing. Thus, a southwesterly wind (from the southwest) has both northward and eastward (to the north and to the east) components. Except near mountains, wind cannot blow up or down near the ground, so the vertical component of wind often is approximated as zero, and the horizontal component is emphasized.

D.1.10. Frozen Precipitation

Frozen precipitation is more difficult to measure than liquid precipitation, especially with automated techniques. Sevruk and Harmon (1984), Goodison et al. (1998), and Yang et al. (1998; 2001) provide many of the reasons to explain this. The importance of frozen precipitation varies greatly from one setting to another. This subject was discussed in greater detail in a related inventory and monitoring report for the Alaska park units (Redmond et al. 2005).

In climates that receive frozen precipitation, a decision must be made whether or not to try to record such events accurately. This usually means that the precipitation must be turned into liquid either by falling into an antifreeze fluid solution that is then weighed or by heating the precipitation enough to melt and fall through a measuring mechanism such as a nearly-balanced tipping bucket. Accurate measurements from the first approach require expensive gauges; tipping buckets can achieve this resolution readily but are more apt to lose some or all precipitation. Improvements have been made to the heating mechanism on the NWS tipping-bucket gauge used for the ASOS to correct its numerous deficiencies making it less problematic; however, this gauge is not inexpensive. A heat supply needed to melt frozen precipitation usually requires more energy than renewable energy (solar panels or wind recharging) can provide thus AC power is needed. Periods of frozen precipitation or rime often provide less-than-optimal recharging conditions with heavy clouds, short days, low-solar-elevation angles and more horizon blocking, and cold temperatures causing additional drain on the battery.

D.1.11. Save or Lose

A second consideration with precipitation is determining if the measurement should be saved (as in weighing systems) or lost (as in tipping-bucket systems). With tipping buckets, after the water has passed through the tipping mechanism, it usually just drops to the ground. Thus, there is no checksum to ensure that the sum of all the tips adds up to what has been saved in a reservoir at some location. By contrast, the weighing gauges continually accumulate until the reservoir is emptied, the reported value is the total reservoir content (for example, the height of the liquid column in a tube), and the incremental precipitation is the difference in depth between two known times. These weighing gauges do not always have the same fine resolution. Some gauges only record to the nearest centimeter, which is usually acceptable for hydrology but not necessarily for other needs. (For reference, a millimeter of precipitation can get a person in street clothes quite wet.) Other weighing gauges are capable of measuring to the 0.25-mm (0.01-in.) resolution but do not have as much capacity and must be emptied more often. Day/night and storm-related thermal expansion and contraction and sometimes wind shaking can cause fluid pressure from accumulated totals to go up and down in SNOTEL gauges by small increments (commonly 0.3-3 cm, or 0.01–0.10 ft) leading to "negative precipitation" followed by similarly non-real light precipitation when, in fact, no change took place in the amount of accumulated precipitation.

D.1.12. Time

Time should always be in local standard time (LST), and daylight savings time (DST) should never be used under any circumstances with automated equipment and timers. Using DST leads to one duplicate hour, one missing hour, and a season of displaced values, as well as needless confusion and a data-management nightmare. Absolute time, such as Greenwich Mean Time (GMT) or Coordinated Universal Time (UTC), also can be used because these formats are unambiguously translatable. Since measurements only provide information about what already *has* occurred or *is* occurring and not what *will* occur, they should always be assigned to the *ending time* of the associated interval with hour 24 marking the end of the last hour of the day. In this system, midnight always represents the end of the day, not the start. To demonstrate the importance of this differentiation, we have encountered situations where police officers seeking corroborating weather data could not recall whether the time on their crime report from a year ago was the starting midnight or the ending midnight! Station positions should be known to within a few meters, easily accomplished with GPS (Global Positioning System), so that time zones and solar angles can be determined accurately.

D.1.13. Automated versus Manual

Most of this report has addressed automated measurements. Historically, most measurements are manual and typically collected once a day. In many cases, manual measurements continue because of habit, usefulness, and desire for continuity over time. Manual measurements are extremely useful and when possible should be encouraged. However, automated measurements are becoming more common. For either, it is important to record time in a logically consistent manner.

It should not be automatically assumed that newer data and measurements are "better" than older data or that manual data are "worse" than automated data. Older or simpler manual measurements are often of very high quality even if they sometimes are not in the most convenient digital format.

There is widespread desire to use automated systems to reduce human involvement. This is admirable and understandable, but every automated weather/climate station or network requires significant human attention and maintenance. A telling example concerns the Oklahoma Mesonet (see Brock et al. 1995, and bibliography at http://www.mesonet.ou.edu), a network of about 115 high–quality, automated meteorological stations spread over Oklahoma, where about 80 percent of the annual ($2–3M) budget is nonetheless allocated to humans with only about 20 percent allocated to equipment.

D.1.14. Manual Conventions

Manual measurements typically are made once a day. Elements usually consist of maximum and minimum temperature, temperature at observation time, precipitation, snowfall, snow depth, and sometimes evaporation, wind, or other information. Since it is not actually known when extremes occurred, the only logical approach, and the nationwide convention, is to ascribe the entire measurement to the time-interval date and to enter it on the form in that way. For morning observers (for example, 8 am to 8 am), this means that the maximum temperature written for today often is from yesterday afternoon and sometimes the minimum temperature for the 24-hr period actually occurred yesterday morning. However, this is understood and expected. It is often a surprise to observers to see how many maximum temperatures do not occur in the afternoon and how many minimum temperatures do not occur in the predawn hours. This is especially true in environments that are colder, higher, northerly, cloudy, mountainous, or coastal. As long as this convention is strictly followed every day, it has been shown that truly excellent climate records can result (Redmond 1992). Manual observers should reset equipment only one time per day at the official observing time. Making more than one measurement a day is discouraged strongly; this practice results in a hybrid record that is too difficult to interpret. The only exception is for total daily snowfall. New snowfall can be measured up to four times per day with no observations closer than six hours. It is well known that more frequent measurement of snow increases the annual total because compaction is a continuous process.

Two main purposes for climate observations are to establish the long-term averages for given locations and to track variations in climate. Broadly speaking, these purposes address topics of absolute and relative climate behavior. Once absolute behavior has been "established" (a task that is never finished because long-term averages continue to vary in time)—temporal variability quickly becomes the item of most interest.

D.2. Representativeness

Having discussed important factors to consider when new sites are installed, we now turn our attention to site "representativeness." In popular usage, we often encounter the notion that a site is "representative" of another site if it receives the same annual precipitation or records the same annual temperature or if some other element-specific, long-term average has a similar value. This notion of representativeness has a certain limited validity, but there are other aspects of this idea that need to be considered.

A climate monitoring site also can be said to be representative if climate records from that site show sufficiently strong temporal correlations with a large number of locations over a sufficiently large area. If station A receives 20 cm a year and station B receives 200 cm a year, these climates obviously receive quite differing amounts of precipitation. However, if their monthly, seasonal, or annual correlations are high (for example, 0.80 or higher for a particular time scale), one site can be used as a surrogate for estimating values at the other if measurements for a particular month, season, or year are missing. That is, a wet or dry month at one station is also a wet or dry month (relative to its own mean) at the comparison station. Note that high correlations on one time scale do not imply automatically that high correlations will occur on other time scales.

Likewise, two stations having similar mean climates (for example, similar annual precipitation) might not co-vary in close synchrony (for example, coastal versus interior). This may be considered a matter of climate "affiliation" for a particular location.

Thus, the representativeness of a site can refer either to the basic climatic averages for a given duration (or time window within the annual cycle) or to the extent that the site co-varies in time with respect to all surrounding locations. One site can be representative of another in the first sense but not the second, or vice versa, or neither, or both—all combinations are possible.

If two sites are perfectly correlated then, in a sense, they are "redundant." However, redundancy has value because all sites will experience missing data especially with automated equipment in rugged environments and harsh climates where outages and other problems nearly can be guaranteed. In many cases, those outages are caused by the weather, particularly by unusual weather and the very conditions we most wish to know about. Methods for filling in those values will require proxy information from this or other nearby networks. Thus, redundancy is a virtue rather than a vice.

In general, the cooperative stations managed by the NWS have produced much longer records than automated stations like RAWS or SNOTEL stations. The RAWS stations often have problems with precipitation, especially in winter, or with missing data, so that low correlations may be data problems rather than climatic dissimilarity. The RAWS records also are relatively short, so correlations should be interpreted with care. In performing and interpreting such analyses, however, we must remember that there are physical climate reasons and observational reasons why stations within a short distance (even a few tens or hundreds of meters) may not correlate well.

D.2.1. Temporal Behavior

It is possible that high correlations will occur between station pairs during certain portions of the year (i.e., January) but low correlations may occur during other portions of the year (e.g., September or October). The relative contributions of these seasons to the annual total (for precipitation) or average (for temperature) and the correlations for each month are both factors in the correlation of an aggregated time window of longer duration that encompasses those seasons (e.g., one of the year definitions such as calendar year or water year). A complete and careful evaluation ideally would include such a correlation analysis but requires more resources and data. Note that it also is possible and frequently is observed that temperatures are highly correlated while precipitation is not or vice versa, and these relations can change according to the time of year. If two stations are well correlated for all climate elements for all portions of the year, then they can be considered redundant.

With scarce resources, the initial strategy should be to try to identify locations that do not correlate particularly well, so that each new site measures something new that cannot be guessed easily from the behavior of surrounding sites. (An important caveat here is that lack of such correlation could be a result of physical climate behavior and not a result of faults with the actual measuring process; i.e., by unrepresentative or simply poor-quality data. Unfortunately, we seldom have perfect climate data.) As additional sites are added, we usually wish for some combination of unique and redundant sites to meet what amounts to essentially orthogonal constraints: new information and more reliably-furnished information.

A common consideration is whether to observe on a ridge or in a valley, given the resources to place a single station within a particular area of a few square kilometers. Ridge and valley stations will correlate very well for temperatures when lapse conditions prevail, particularly summer daytime temperatures. In summer at night or winter at daylight, the picture will be more mixed and correlations will be lower. In winter at night when inversions are common and even the rule, correlations may be zero or even negative and perhaps even more divergent as the two sites are on opposite sides of the inversion. If we had the luxury of locating stations everywhere, we would find that ridge tops generally correlate very well with other ridge tops and similarly valleys with other valleys, but ridge tops correlate well with valleys only under certain circumstances. Beyond this, valleys and ridges having similar orientations usually will correlate better with each other than those with perpendicular orientations, depending on their orientation with respect to large-scale wind flow and solar angles.

Unfortunately, we do not have stations everywhere, so we are forced to use the few comparisons that we have and include a large dose of intelligent reasoning, using what we have observed elsewhere. In performing and interpreting such analyses, we must remember that there are physical climatic reasons and observational reasons why stations within a short distance (even a few tens or hundreds of meters) may not correlate well.

Examples of correlation analyses include those for the Channel Islands and for southwest Alaska, which can be found in Redmond and McCurdy (2005) and Redmond et al. (2005). These examples illustrate what can be learned from correlation analyses. Spatial correlations generally vary by time of year. Thus, results should be displayed in the form of annual correlation cycles—for monthly mean temperature and monthly total precipitation and perhaps other climate elements like wind or humidity—between station pairs selected for climatic setting and data availability and quality.

In general, the COOP stations managed by the NWS have produced much longer records than have automated stations like RAWS or SNOTEL stations. The RAWS stations also often have problems with precipitation, especially in winter or with missing data, so that low correlations may be data problems rather than climate dissimilarity. The RAWS records are much shorter, so correlations should be interpreted with care, but these stations are more likely to be in places of interest for remote or under-sampled regions.

D.2.2. Spatial Behavior

A number of techniques exist to interpolate from isolated point values to a spatial domain. For example, a common technique is simple inverse distance weighting. Critical to the success of the simplest of such techniques is that some other property of the spatial domain, one that is influential for the mapped element, does not vary significantly. Topography greatly influences precipitation, temperature, wind, humidity, and most other meteorological elements. Thus, this criterion clearly is not met in any region having extreme topographic diversity. In such circumstances, simple Cartesian distance may have little to do with how rapidly correlation deteriorates from one site to the next, and in fact, the correlations can decrease readily from a mountain to a valley and then increase again on the next mountain. Such structure in the fields of spatial correlation is not seen in the relatively (statistically) well-behaved flat areas like those in the eastern United States.

To account for dominating effects such as topography and inland–coastal differences that exist in certain regions, some kind of additional knowledge must be brought to bear to produce meaningful, physically plausible, and observationally based interpolations. Historically, this has proven to be an extremely difficult problem, especially to perform objective and repeatable analyses. An analysis performed for southwest Alaska (Redmond et al. 2005) concluded that the PRISM maps (Daly et al. 1994, Daly et al. 2002; Gibson et al. 2002; Doggett et al. 2004) were probably the best available. An analysis by Simpson et al. (2005) further discussed many issues in the mapping of Alaska's climate and resulted in the same conclusion about PRISM.

D.2.3. Climate-Change Detection

Although general purpose climate stations should be situated to address all aspects of climate variability, it is desirable that they also be in locations that are more sensitive to climate change from natural or anthropogenic influences should it begin to occur. The question here is how well we know such sensitivities. The climate-change issue is quite complex because it encompasses more than just greenhouse gasses.

Sites that are in locations or climates particularly vulnerable to climate change should be favored. How this vulnerability is determined is a considerably challenging research issue. Candidate locations or situations are those that lie on the border between two major biomes or just inside the edge of one or the other. In these cases, a slight movement of the boundary in anticipated direction (toward "warmer," for example) would be much easier to detect as the boundary moves past the site and a different set of biota begin to be established. Such a vegetative or ecologic response would be more visible and would take less time to establish as a real change than would a smaller change in the center of the distribution range of a marker or key species.

D.2.4. Element-Specific Differences

The various climate elements (temperature, precipitation, cloudiness, snowfall, humidity, wind speed and direction, solar radiation) do not vary through time in the same sequence or manner nor should they necessarily be expected to vary in this manner. The spatial patterns of variability should not be expected to be the same for all elements. These patterns also should not be expected to be similar for all months or seasons. The suitability of individual sites for measurement also varies from one element to another. A site that has a favorable exposure for temperature or wind may not have a favorable exposure for precipitation or snowfall. A site that experiences proper air movement may be situated in a topographic channel, such as a river valley or a pass, which restricts the range of wind directions and affects the distribution of speed-direction categories.

D.2.5. Logistics and Practical Factors

Even with the most advanced scientific rationale, sites in some remote or climatically challenging settings may not be suitable because of the difficulty in servicing and maintaining equipment. Contributing to these challenges are scheduling difficulties, animal behavior, snow burial, icing, snow behavior, access and logistical problems, and the weather itself. Remote and elevated sites usually require far more attention and expense than a rain-dominated, easily accessible valley location.

For climate purposes, station exposure and the local environment should be maintained in their original state (vegetation especially), so that changes seen are the result of regional climate variations and not of trees growing up, bushes crowding a site, surface albedo changing, fire clearing, etc. Repeat photography has shown many examples of slow environmental change in the vicinity of a station in rather short time frames (5–20 years), and this technique should be employed routinely and frequently at all locations. In the end, logistics, maintenance, and other practical factors almost always determine the success of weather- and climate-monitoring activities.

D.2.6. Personnel Factors

Many past experiences (almost exclusively negative) strongly support the necessity to place primary responsibility for station deployment and maintenance in the hands of seasoned, highly qualified, trained, and meticulously careful personnel, the more experienced the better. Over time, even in "benign" climates but especially where harsher conditions prevail, every conceivable problem will occur and both the usual and unusual should be anticipated: weather, animals, plants, salt, sensor and communication failure, windblown debris, corrosion, power failures, vibrations, avalanches, snow loading and creep, corruption of the data logger program, etc. An ability to anticipate and forestall such problems, a knack for innovation and improvisation, knowledge of electronics, practical and organizational skills, and presence of mind to bring the various small but vital parts, spares, tools, and diagnostic troubleshooting equipment are highly valued qualities. Especially when logistics are so expensive, a premium should be placed on using experienced personnel, since the slightest and seemingly most minor mistake can render a station useless or, even worse, uncertain. Exclusive reliance on individuals without this background can be costly and almost always will result eventually in unnecessary loss of data. Skilled labor and an apprenticeship system to develop new skilled labor will greatly reduce (but not eliminate) the types of problems that can occur in operating a climate network.

D.3. Site Selection
In addition to considerations identified previously in this appendix, various factors need to be considered in selecting sites for new or augmented instrumentation.

D.3.1. Equipment and Exposure Factors
D.3.1.1. Measurement Suite: All sites should measure temperature, humidity, wind, solar radiation, and snow depth. Precipitation measurements are more difficult but probably should be attempted with the understanding that winter measurements may be of limited or no value unless an all-weather gauge has been installed. Even if an all-weather gauge has been installed, it is desirable to have a second gauge present that operates on a different principle–for example, a fluid-based system like those used in the SNOTEL stations in tandem with a higher–resolution, tipping bucket gauge for summertime. Without heating, a tipping bucket gauge usually is of use only when temperatures are above freezing and when temperatures have not been below freezing for some time, so that accumulated ice and snow is not melting and being recorded as present precipitation. Gauge undercatch is a significant issue in snowy climates, so shielding should be considered for all gauges designed to work over the winter months. It is very important to note the presence or absence of shielding, the type of shielding, and the dates of installation or removal of the shielding.

D.3.1.2. Overall Exposure: The ideal, general all-purpose site has gentle slopes, is open to the sun and the wind, has a natural vegetative cover, avoids strong local (less than 200 m) influences, and represents a reasonable compromise among all climate elements. The best temperature sites are not the best precipitation sites, and the same is true for other elements. Steep topography in the immediate vicinity should be avoided unless settings where precipitation is affected by steep topography are being deliberately sought or a mountaintop or ridgeline is the desired location. The potential for disturbance should be considered: fire and flood risk, earth movement, wind-borne debris, volcanic deposits or lahars, vandalism, animal tampering, and general human encroachment are all factors.

D.3.1.3. Elevation: Mountain climates do not vary in time in exactly the same manner as adjoining valley climates. This concept is emphasized when temperature inversions are present to a greater degree and during precipitation when winds rise up the slopes at the same angle. There is considerable concern that mountain climates will be (or already are) changing and perhaps changing differently than lowland climates, which has direct and indirect consequences for plant and animal life in the more extreme zones. Elevations of special significance are those that are near the mean rain/snow line for winter, near the tree line, and near the mean annual freezing level (all of these may not be quite the same). Because the lapse rates in wet climates often are nearly moist-adiabatic during the main precipitation seasons, measurements at one elevation may be extrapolated to nearby elevations. In drier climates and in the winter, temperature and to a lesser extent wind will show various elevation profiles.

D.3.1.4. Transects: The concept of observing transects that span climatic gradients is sound. This is not always straightforward in topographically uneven terrain, but these transects could still be arranged by setting up station(s) along the coast; in or near passes atop the main coastal interior drainage divide; and inland at one, two, or three distances into the interior lowlands. Transects need not—and by dint of topographic constraints probably cannot—be straight lines, but the closer that a line can be approximated the better. The main point is to systematically sample the key points of a behavioral transition without deviating too radically from linearity.

D.3.1.5. Other Topographic Considerations: There are various considerations with respect to local topography. Local topography can influence wind (channeling, upslope/downslope, etc.), precipitation (orographic enhancement, downslope evaporation, catch efficiency, etc.), and temperature (frost pockets, hilltops, aspect, mixing or decoupling from the overlying atmosphere, bowls, radiative effects, etc.), to different degrees at differing scales. In general, for measurements to be areally representative, it is better to avoid these local effects to the extent that they can be identified before station deployment (once deployed, it is desirable not to move a station). The primary purpose of a climate-monitoring network should be to serve as an infrastructure in the form of a set of benchmark stations for comparing other stations. Sometimes, however, it is exactly these local phenomena that we want to capture. Living organisms, especially plants, are affected by their immediate environment, whether it is representative of a larger setting or not. Specific measurements of limited scope and duration made for these purposes then can be tied to the main benchmarks. This experience is useful also in determining the complexity needed in the benchmark monitoring process in order to capture particular phenomena at particular space and time scales.

Sites that drain (cold air) well generally are better than sites that allow cold air to pool. Slightly sloped areas (1 degree is fine) or small benches from tens to hundreds of meters above streams are often favorable locations. Furthermore, these sites often tend to be out of the path of hazards (like floods) and to have rocky outcroppings where controlling vegetation will not be a major concern. Benches or wide spots on the rise between two forks of a river system are often the only flat areas and sometimes jut out to give greater exposure to winds from more directions.

D.3.1.6. Prior History: The starting point in designing a program is to determine what kinds of observations have been collected over time, by whom, in what manner, and if these observation are continuing to the present time. It also may be of value to "re-occupy" the former site of a station that is now inactive to provide some measure of continuity or a reference point from the past. This can be of value even if continuous observations were not made during the entire intervening period.

D.3.2. Element-Specific Factors

D.3.2.1. Temperature: An open exposure with uninhibited air movement is the preferred setting. The most common measurement is made at approximately eye level, 1.5–2.0 m. In snowy locations sensors should be at least one meter higher than the deepest snowpack expected in the next 50 years or perhaps 2–3 times the depth of the average maximum annual depth. Sensors should be shielded above and below from solar radiation (bouncing off snow), from sunrise/sunset horizontal input, and from vertical rock faces. Sensors should be clamped tightly, so that they do not swivel away from level stacks of radiation plates. Nearby vegetation should be kept away from the sensors (several meters). Growing vegetation should be cut to original conditions. Small hollows and swales can cool tremendously at night, and it is best avoid these areas. Side slopes of perhaps a degree or two of angle facilitate air movement and drainage and, in effect, sample a large area during nighttime hours. The very bottom of a valley should be avoided. Temperature can change substantially from moves of only a few meters. Situations have been observed where flat and seemingly uniform conditions (like airport runways) appear to demonstrate different climate behaviors over short distances of a few tens or hundreds of meters (differences of 5–10°C). When snow is on the ground, these microclimatic differences can be stronger, and differences of 2–5°C can occur in the short distance between the thermometer and the snow surface on calm evenings.

D.3.2.2. Precipitation (liquid): Calm locations with vegetative or artificial shielding are preferred. Wind will adversely impact readings; therefore, the less the better. Wind effects on precipitation are far less for rain than for snow. Devices that "save" precipitation present advantages, but most gauges are built to dump precipitation as it falls or to empty periodically. Automated gauges give both the amount and the timing. Simple backups that record only the total precipitation since the last visit have a certain advantage (for example, storage gauges or lengths of PVC pipe perhaps with bladders on the bottom). The following question should be asked: Does the total precipitation from an automated gauge add up to the measured total in a simple bucket (evaporation is prevented with an appropriate substance such as mineral oil)? Drip from overhanging foliage and trees can augment precipitation totals.

D.3.2.3. Precipitation (frozen): Calm locations or shielding are a must. Undercatch for rain is only about 5 percent, but with winds of only 2–4 m/s, gauges may catch only 30–70 percent of the actual snow falling depending on density of the flakes. To catch 100 percent of the snow, the standard configuration for shielding is employed by the CRN (Climate Reference Network): the DFIR (Double-Fence Intercomparison Reference) shield with 2.4-m (8-ft.) vertical, wooden slatted fences in two concentric octagons with diameters of 8 m and 4 m (26 ft and 13 ft, respectively) and an inner Alter shield (flapping vanes). Numerous tests have shown this is the only way to achieve complete catch of snowfall (Yang et al. 1998; 2001). The DFIR shield is large and bulky; it is recommended that all precipitation gauges have at least Alter shields on them.

Near oceans, much snow is heavy and falls more vertically. In colder locations or storms, light flakes frequently will fly in and then out of the gauge. Clearings in forests are usually excellent sites. Snow blowing from trees that are too close can augment actual precipitation totals. Artificial shielding (vanes, etc.) placed around gauges in snowy locales always should be used if accurate totals are desired. Moving parts tend to freeze up. Capping of gauges during heavy snowfall events is a common occurrence. When the cap becomes pointed, snow falls off to the ground and is not recorded. Caps and plugs often will not fall into the tube until hours, days, or even weeks have passed, typically during an extended period of freezing temperature or above or when sunlight finally occurs. Liquid-based measurements (e.g., SNOTEL "rocket" gauges) do not have the resolution (usually 0.3 cm [0.1 in.] rather than 0.03 cm [0.01 in.]) that tipping bucket and other gauges have but are known to be reasonably accurate in very snowy climates. Light snowfall events might not be recorded until enough of them add up to the next reporting increment. More expensive gauges like Geonors can be considered and could do quite well in snowy settings; however, they need to be emptied every 40 cm (15 in.) or so (capacity of 51 cm [20 in.]) until the new 91-cm (36-in.) capacity gauge is offered for sale. Recently, the NWS has been trying out the new (and very expensive) Ott all-weather gauge. Riming can be an issue in windy foggy environments below freezing. Rime, dew, and other forms of atmospheric condensation are not real precipitation, since they are caused by the gauge.

D.3.2.4. Snow Depth: Windswept areas tend to be blown clear of snow. Conversely, certain types of vegetation can act as a snow fence and cause artificial drifts. However, some amount of vegetation in the vicinity generally can help slow down the wind. The two most common types of snow-depth gauges are the Judd Snow Depth Sensor, produced by Judd Communications, and the snow depth gauge produced by Campbell Scientific, Inc. Opinions vary on which one is better. These gauges use ultrasound and look downward in a cone about 22 degrees in diameter. The ground should be relatively clear of vegetation and maintained in a manner so that the zero point on the calibration scale does not change.

D.3.2.5. Snow Water Equivalent: This is determined by the weight of snow on fluid-filled pads about the size of a desktop set up sometimes in groups of four or in larger hexagons several meters in diameter. These pads require flat ground some distance from nearby sources of windblown snow and shielding that is "just right": not too close to the shielding to act as a kind of snow fence and not too far from the shielding so that blowing and drifting become a factor. Generally, these pads require fluids that possess antifreeze-like properties, as well as handling and replacement protocols.

D.3.2.6. Wind: Open exposures are needed for wind measurements. Small prominences or benches without blockage from certain sectors are preferred. A typical rule for trees is to site stations back 10 tree-heights from all tree obstructions. Sites in long, narrow valleys can obviously only exhibit two main wind directions. Gently rounded eminences are more favored. Any kind of topographic steering should be avoided to the extent possible. Avoiding major mountain chains or single isolated mountains or ridges is usually a favorable approach, if there is a choice. Sustained wind speed and the highest gusts (1-second) should be recorded. Averaging methodologies for both sustained winds and gusts can affect climate trends and should be recorded as metadata with all changes noted. Vegetation growth affects the vertical wind profile, and growth over a few years can lead to changes in mean wind speed even if the "real" wind does not change, so vegetation near the site (perhaps out to 50 m) should be maintained in a quasi-permanent status (same height and spatial distribution). Wind devices can rime up and freeze or spin out of balance. In severely rimed or windy climates, rugged anemometers, such as those made by Taylor, are worth considering. These anemometers are expensive but durable and can withstand substantial abuse. In exposed locations, personnel should plan for winds to be at least 50 m/s and be able to measure these wind speeds. At a minimum, anemometers should be rated to 75 m/s.

D.3.2.7. Humidity: Humidity is a relatively straightforward climate element. Close proximity to lakes or other water features can affect readings. Humidity readings typically are less accurate near 100 percent and at low humidities in cold weather.

D.3.2.8. Solar Radiation: A site with an unobstructed horizon obviously is the most desirable. This generally implies a flat plateau or summit. However, in most locations trees or mountains will obstruct the sun for part of the day.

D.3.2.9. Soil Temperature: It is desirable to measure soil temperature at locations where soil is present. If soil temperature is recorded at only a single depth, the most preferred depth is 10 cm. Other common depths include 25 cm, 50 cm, 2 cm, and 100 cm. Biological activity in the soil will be proportional to temperature with important threshold effects occurring near freezing.

D.3.2.10. Soil Moisture: Soil-moisture gauges are somewhat temperamental and require care to install. The soil should be characterized by a soil expert during installation of the gauge. The readings may require a certain level of experience to interpret correctly. If accurate, readings of soil moisture are especially useful.

D.3.2.11. Distributed Observations: It can be seen readily that compromises must be struck among the considerations described in the preceding paragraphs because some are mutually exclusive.

How large can a "site" be? Generally, the equipment footprint should be kept as small as practical with all components placed next to each other (within less than 10–20 m or so). Readings from one instrument frequently are used to aid in interpreting readings from the remaining instruments.

What is a tolerable degree of separation? Some consideration may be given to locating a precipitation gauge or snow pillow among protective vegetation, while the associated temperature, wind, and humidity readings would be collected more effectively in an open and exposed location within 20–50 m. Ideally, it is advantageous to know the wind measurement precisely at the precipitation gauge, but a compromise involving a short split, and in effect a "distributed observation," could be considered. There are no definitive rules governing this decision, but it is suggested that the site footprint be kept within approximately 50 m. There also are constraints imposed by engineering and electrical factors that affect cable lengths, signal strength, and line noise; therefore, the shorter the cable the better. Practical issues include the need to trench a channel to outlying instruments or to allow lines to lie atop the ground and associated problems with animals, humans, weathering, etc. Separating a precipitation gauge up to 100 m or so from an instrument mast may be an acceptable compromise if other factors are not limiting.

D.3.2.12. Instrument Replacement Schedules: Instruments slowly degrade, and a plan for replacing them with new, refurbished, or recalibrated instruments should be in place. After approximately five years, a systematic change-out procedure should result in replacing most sensors in a network. Certain parts, such as solar radiation sensors, are candidates for annual calibration or change-out. Anemometers tend to degrade as bearings erode or electrical contacts become uneven. Noisy bearings are an indication, and a stethoscope might aid in hearing such noises. Increased internal friction affects the threshold starting speed; once spinning, they tend to function properly. Increases in starting threshold speeds can lead to more zero-wind measurements and thus reduce the reported mean wind speed with no real change in wind properties. A field calibration kit should be developed and taken on all site visits, routine or otherwise. Rain gauges can be tested with drip testers during field visits. Protective conduit and tight water seals can prevent abrasion and moisture problems with the equipment, although seals can keep moisture in as well as out. Bulletproof casings sometimes are employed in remote settings. A supply of spare parts, at least one of each and more for less-expensive or more-delicate sensors, should be maintained to allow replacement of worn or nonfunctional instruments during field visits. In addition, this approach allows instruments to be calibrated in the relative convenience of the operational home—the larger the network, the greater the need for a parts depot.

D.3.3. Long-Term Comparability and Consistency

D.3.3.1. Consistency: The emphasis here is to hold biases constant. Every site has biases, problems, and idiosyncrasies of one sort or another. The best rule to follow is simply to try to keep biases constant through time. Since the goal is to track climate through time, keeping sensors, methodologies, and exposure constant will ensure that only true climate change is being measured. This means leaving the site in its original state or performing maintenance to keep it that way. Once a site is installed, the goal should be to never move the site even by a few meters or to allow significant changes to occur within 100 m for the next several decades.

Sites in or near rock outcroppings likely will experience less vegetative disturbance or growth through the years and will not usually retain moisture, a factor that could speed corrosion. Sites that will remain locally similar for some time are usually preferable. However, in some cases the intent of a station might be to record the local climate effects of changes within a small-scale system (for example, glacier, recently burned area, or scene of some other disturbance) that is subject to a regional climate influence. In this example, the local changes might be much larger than the regional changes.

D.3.3.2. Metadata: Since the climate of every site is affected by features in the immediate vicinity, it is vital to record this information over time and to update the record repeatedly at each service visit. Distances, angles, heights of vegetation, fine-scale topography, condition of instruments, shielding discoloration, and other factors from within a meter to several kilometers should be noted. Systematic photography should be undertaken and updated at least once every one–two years.

Photographic documentation should be taken at each site in a standard manner and repeated every two–three years. Guidelines for methodology were developed by Redmond (2004) as a result of experience with the NOAA CRN and can be found on the WRCC NPS Web pages at http://www.wrcc.dri.edu/nps and at ftp://ftp.wrcc.dri.edu/nps/photodocumentation.pdf.

The main purpose for climate stations is to *track climatic conditions through time*. Anything that affects the interpretation of records through time must to be noted and recorded for posterity. The important factors should be clear to a person who has never visited the site, no matter how long ago the site was installed.

In regions with significant, climatic transition zones, transects are an efficient way to span several climates and make use of available resources. Discussions on this topic at greater detail can be found in Redmond and Simeral (2004) and in Redmond et al. (2005).

D.4. Literature Cited

American Association of State Climatologists. 1985. Heights and exposure standards for sensors on automated weather stations. The State Climatologist **9**.

Brock, F. V., K. C. Crawford, R. L. Elliott, G. W. Cuperus, S. J. Stadler, H. L. Johnson and M. D. Eilts. 1995. The Oklahoma Mesonet: A technical overview. Journal of Atmospheric and Oceanic Technology **12**:5-19.

Daly, C., R. P. Neilson, and D. L. Phillips. 1994. A statistical-topographic model for mapping climatological precipitation over mountainous terrain. Journal of Applied Meteorology **33**:140-158.

Daly, C., W. P. Gibson, G. H. Taylor, G. L. Johnson, and P. Pasteris. 2002. A knowledge-based approach to the statistical mapping of climate. Climate Research **22**:99-113.

Doggett, M., C. Daly, J. Smith, W. Gibson, G. Taylor, G. Johnson, and P. Pasteris. 2004. High-resolution 1971-2000 mean monthly temperature maps for the western United States. Fourteenth AMS Conf. on Applied Climatology, 84th AMS Annual Meeting. Seattle, WA, American Meteorological Society, Boston, MA, January 2004, Paper 4.3, CD-ROM.

Geiger, R., R. H. Aron, and P. E. Todhunter. 2003. The Climate Near the Ground. 6th edition. Rowman & Littlefield Publishers, Inc., New York.

Gibson, W. P., C. Daly, T. Kittel, D. Nychka, C. Johns, N. Rosenbloom, A. McNab, and G. Taylor. 2002. Development of a 103-year high-resolution climate data set for the conterminous United States. Thirteenth AMS Conf. on Applied Climatology. Portland, OR, American Meteorological Society, Boston, MA, May 2002:181-183.

Goodison, B. E., P. Y. T. Louie, and D. Yang. 1998. WMO solid precipitation measurement intercomparison final report. WMO TD 982, World Meteorological Organization, Geneva, Switzerland.

National Research Council. 1998. Future of the National Weather Service Cooperative Weather Network. National Academies Press, Washington, D.C.

National Research Council. 2001. A Climate Services Vision: First Steps Toward the Future. National Academies Press, Washington, D.C.

Redmond, K. T. 1992. Effects of observation time on interpretation of climatic time series - A need for consistency. Eighth Annual Pacific Climate (PACLIM) Workshop. Pacific Grove, CA, March 1991:141-150.

Redmond, K. T. 2004. Photographic documentation of long-term climate stations. Available from ftp://ftp.wrcc.dri.edu/nps/photodocumentation.pdf. (accessed 15 August 2004)

Redmond, K. T. and D. B. Simeral. 2004. Climate monitoring comments: Central Alaska Network Inventory and Monitoring Program. Available from ftp://ftp.wrcc.dri.edu/nps/alaska/cakn/npscakncomments040406.pdf. (accessed 6 April 2004)

Redmond, K. T., D. B. Simeral, and G. D. McCurdy. 2005. Climate monitoring for southwest Alaska national parks: network design and site selection. Report 05-01. Western Regional Climate Center, Reno, Nevada.

Redmond, K. T., and G. D. McCurdy. 2005. Channel Islands National Park: Design considerations for weather and climate monitoring. Report 05-02. Western Regional Climate Center, Reno, Nevada.

Sevruk, B., and W. R. Hamon. 1984. International comparison of national precipitation gauges with a reference pit gauge. Instruments and Observing Methods, Report No 17, WMO/TD – 38, World Meteorological Organization, Geneva, Switzerland.

Simpson, J. J., Hufford, G. L., C. Daly, J. S. Berg, and M. D. Fleming. 2005. Comparing maps of mean monthly surface temperature and precipitation for Alaska and adjacent areas of Canada produced by two different methods. Arctic **58**:137-161.

Whiteman, C. D. 2000. Mountain Meteorology: Fundamentals and Applications. Oxford University Press, Oxford, UK.

Wilson, E. O. 1998. Consilience: The Unity of Knowledge. Knopf, New York.

World Meteorological Organization. 1983. Guide to meteorological instruments and methods of observation, No. 8, 5th edition, World Meteorological Organization, Geneva Switzerland.

World Meteorological Organization. 2005. Organization and planning of intercomparisons of rainfall intensity gauges. World Meteorological Organization, Geneva Switzerland.

Yang, D., B. E. Goodison, J. R. Metcalfe, V. S. Golubev, R. Bates, T. Pangburn, and C. Hanson. 1998. Accuracy of NWS 8" standard nonrecording precipitation gauge: results and application of WMO intercomparison. Journal of Atmospheric and Oceanic Technology **15**:54-68.

Yang, D., B. E. Goodison, J. R. Metcalfe, P. Louie, E. Elomaa, C. Hanson, V. Bolubev, T. Gunther, J. Milkovic, and M. Lapin. 2001. Compatibility evaluation of national precipitation gauge measurements. Journal of Geophysical Research **106**:1481-1491.

Appendix E. Master metadata field list

Field Name	Field Type	Field Description
begin_date	date	Effective beginning date for a record.
begin_date_flag	char(2)	Flag describing the known accuracy of the begin date for a station.
best_elevation	float(4)	Best known elevation for a station (in feet).
clim_div_code	char(2)	Foreign key defining climate division code (primary in table: clim_div).
clim_div_key	int2	Foreign key defining climate division for a station (primary in table: clim_div.
clim_div_name	varchar(30)	English name for a climate division.
controller_info	varchar(50)	Person or organization who maintains the identifier system for a given weather or climate network.
country_key	int2	Foreign key defining country where a station resides (primary in table: none).
county_key	int2	Foreign key defining county where a station resides (primary in table: county).
county_name	varchar(31)	English name for a county.
description	text	Any description pertaining to the particular table.
end_date	date	Last effective date for a record.
end_date_flag	char(2)	Flag describing the known accuracy of station end date.
fips_country_code	char(2)	FIPS (federal information processing standards) country code.
fips_state_abbr	char(2)	FIPS state abbreviation for a station.
fips_state_code	char(2)	FIPS state code for a station.
history_flag	char(2)	Describes temporal significance of an individual record among others from the same station.
id_type_key	int2	Foreign key defining the id_type for a station (usually defined in code).
last_updated	date	Date of last update for a record.
latitude	float(8)	Latitude value.
longitude	float(8)	Longitude value.
name_type_key	int2	"3": COOP station name, "2": best station name.
name	varchar(30)	Station name as known at date of last update entry.
ncdc_state_code	char(2)	NCDC, two-character code identifying U.S. state.
network_code	char(8)	Eight-character abbreviation code identifying a network.
network_key	int2	Foreign key defining the network for a station (primary in table: network).
network_station_id	int4	Identifier for a station in the associated network, which is defined by id_type_key.
remark	varchar(254)	Additional information for a record.
src_quality_code	char(2)	Code describing the data quality for the data source.
state_key	int2	Foreign key defining the U.S. state where a station resides (primary in table: state).
state_name	varchar(30)	English name for a state.
station_alt_name	varchar(30)	Other English names for a station.
station_best_name	varchar(30)	Best, most well-known English name for a station.
time_zone	float4	Time zone where a station resides.
ucan_station_id	int4	Unique station identifier for every station in ACIS.
unit_key	int2	Integer value representing a unit of measure.

Field Name	Field Type	Field Description
updated_by	char(8)	Person who last updated a record.
var_major_id	int2	Defines major climate variable.
var_minor_id	int2	Defines data source within a var_major_id.
zipcode	char(5)	Zipcode where a latitude/longitude point resides.
nps_netcode	char(4)	Network four-character identifier.
nps_netname	varchar(128)	Displayed English name for a network.
parkcode	char(4)	Park four-character identifier.
parkname	varchar(128)	Displayed English name for a park/
im_network	char(4)	NPS I&M network where park belongs (a net code)/
station_id	varchar(16)	Station identifier.
station_id_type	varchar(16)	Type of station identifier.
network.subnetwork.id	varchar(16)	Identifier of a sub-network in associated network.
subnetwork_key	int2	Foreign key defining sub-network for a station.
subnetwork_name	varchar(30)	English name for a sub-network.
slope	integer	Terrain slope at the location.
aspect	integer	Terrain aspect at the station.
gps	char(1)	Indicator of latitude/longitude recorded via GPS.
site_description	text(0)	Physical description of site.
route_directions	text(0)	Driving route or site access directions.
station_photo_id	integer	Unique identifier associating a group of photos to a station. Group of photos all taken on same date.
photo_id	char(30)	Unique identifier for a photo.
photo_date	datetime	Date photograph taken.
photographer	varchar(64)	Name of photographer.
maintenance_date	datetime	Date of station maintenance visit.
contact_key	Integer	Unique identifier associating contact information to a station.
full_name	varchar(64)	Full name of contact person.
organization	varchar(64)	Organization of contact person.
contact_type	varchar(32)	Type of contact person (operator, administrator, etc.)
position_title	varchar(32)	Title of contact person.
address	varchar(32)	Address for contact person.
city	varchar(32)	City for contact person.
state	varchar(2)	State for contact person.
zip_code	char(10)	Zipcode for contact person.
country	varchar(32)	Country for contact person.
email	varchar(64)	E-mail for contact person.
work_phone	varchar(16)	Work phone for contact person.
contact_notes	text(254)	Other details regarding contact person.
equipment_type	char(30)	Sensor measurement type; i.e., wind speed, air temperature, etc.
eq_manufacturer	char(30)	Manufacturer of equipment.
eq_model	char(20)	Model number of equipment.
serial_num	char(20)	Serial number of equipment.
eq_description	varchar(254)	Description of equipment.
install_date	datetime	Installation date of equipment.
remove_date	datetime	Removal date of equipment.
ref_height	integer	Sensor displacement height from surface.
sampling_interval	varchar(10)	Frequency of sensor measurement.

Appendix F. Electronic supplements

F.1. ACIS metadata file for weather and climate stations associated with the SIEN:
http://www.wrcc.dri.edu/nps/pub/SIEN/metadata/SIEN_from_ACIS.tar.gz.

F.2. SIEN metadata files for weather and climate stations associated with the SIEN:
http://www.wrcc.dri.edu/nps/pub/SIEN/metadata/SIEN_NPS.tar.gz.

Appendix G. Descriptions of weather/climate monitoring networks

G.1. California Air Resources Board (CARB) Network

- Purpose of network: provide meteorological data in support of air resource monitoring efforts in California.
- Data websites: http://www.met.utah.edu/jhorel/html/mesonet and http://www.arb.ca.gov.
- Measured weather/climate elements:
  - Air temperature.
  - Relative humidity.
  - Precipitation.
  - Wind speed and direction.
- Sampling frequency: hourly.
- Reporting frequency: hourly.
- Estimated station cost: unknown.
- Network strengths:
  - Data are in near-real-time.
  - Extensive coverage in California.
- Network weaknesses:
  - Limited number of meteorological elements.

Meteorological measurements are taken at CARB sites in support of their overall mission of promoting and protecting public health, welfare and ecological resources in California through the reduction of air pollutants, while accounting for economical effects of such measures.

G.2. Clean Air Status and Trends Network (CASTNet)

- Purpose of network: provide information for evaluating the effectiveness of national emission-control strategies.
- Primary management agency: EPA.
- Data website: http://epa.gov/castnet/.
- Measured weather/climate elements:
  - Air temperature.
  - Precipitation.
  - Relative humidity.
  - Wind speed.
  - Wind direction.
  - Wind gust.
  - Gust direction.
  - Solar radiation.
  - Soil moisture and temperature.
- Sampling frequency: hourly.
- Reporting frequency: hourly.
- Estimated station cost: $13000.
- Network strengths:

o High-quality data.
  o Sites are well maintained.
- Network weaknesses:
  o Density of station coverage is low.
  o Shorter periods of record for western United States.

The CASTNet network is primarily is an air-quality-monitoring network managed by the EPA. The elements shown here are intended to support interpretation of measured air-quality parameters such as ozone, nitrates, sulfides, etc., which also are measured at CASTNet sites.

G.3. California Irrigation Management Information System (CIMIS)

- Purpose of network: provide meteorological data to assist in irrigation activities and other water resource management issues for California agricultural interests.
- Primary management agencies: CDWR.
- Data website: http://www.cimis.water.ca.gov/cimis/data.jsp.
- Measured weather/climate elements:
  o Air temperature.
  o Precipitation.
  o Relative humidity.
  o Wind speed and direction.
  o Solar radiation.
  o Soil temperature and moisture (some sites).
- Sampling frequency: hourly.
- Reporting frequency: hourly.
- Estimated station cost: unknown.
- Network strengths:
  o Near-real-time.
  o Sites are generally well-maintained.
  o Data access.
- Network weaknesses:
  o Somewhat limited number of meteorological elements.
  o Coverage limited to California.

The California Irrigation Management Information System (CIMIS), operated through the California Department of Water Resources, is a network of over 120 automated weather stations in the state of California. CIMIS stations are used to assist irrigators in managing their water resources efficiently.

G.4. NWS Cooperative Observer Program (COOP)

- Purpose of network:
  o Provide observational, meteorological data required to define U.S. climate and help measure long-term climate changes.
  o Provide observational, meteorological data in near real-time to support forecasting and warning mechanisms and other public service programs of the NWS.
- Primary management agency: NOAA (NWS).

- Data website: data are available from the NCDC (http://www.ncdc.noaa.gov), RCCs (e.g., WRCC, http://www.wrcc.dri.edu), and state climate offices.
- Measured weather/climate elements:
  - Maximum, minimum, and observation-time temperature.
  - Precipitation, snowfall, snow depth.
  - Pan evaporation (some stations).
- Sampling frequency: daily.
- Reporting frequency: daily or monthly (station-dependent).
- Estimated station cost: $2000 with maintenance costs of $500–900/year.
- Network strengths:
  - Decade–century records at most sites.
  - Widespread national coverage (thousands of stations).
  - Excellent data quality when well maintained.
  - Relatively inexpensive; highly cost effective.
  - Manual measurements; not automated.
- Network weaknesses:
  - Uneven exposures; many are not well-maintained.
  - Dependence on schedules for volunteer observers.
  - Slow entry of data from many stations into national archives.
  - Data subject to observational methodology; not always documented.
  - Manual measurements; not automated and not hourly.

The COOP network has long served as the main climate observation network in the United States. Readings are usually made by volunteers using equipment supplied, installed, and maintained by the federal government. The observer in effect acts as a host for the data-gathering activities and supplies the labor; this is truly a "cooperative" effort. The SAO sites often are considered to be part of the cooperative network as well if they collect the previously mentioned types of weather and climate observations. Typical observation days are morning to morning, evening to evening, or midnight to midnight. By convention, observations are ascribed to the date the instrument was reset at the end of the observational period. For this reason, midnight observations represent the end of a day. The Historical Climate Network is a subset of the cooperative network but contains longer and more complete records.

G.5. Citizen Weather Observer Program (CWOP)

- Purpose of network: collect observations from private citizens and make these data available for homeland security and other weather applications, providing constant feedback to the observers to maintain high data quality.
- Primary management agency: NOAA MADIS program.
- Data Website: http://www.wxqa.com.
- Measured weather/climate elements:
  - Air temperature.
  - Dewpoint temperature.
  - Precipitation.
  - Wind speed and direction.
  - Barometric pressure.

- Sampling frequency: 15 minutes or less.
- Reporting frequency: 15 minutes.
- Estimated station cost: unknown.
- Network strengths:
  o Active partnership between public agencies and private citizens.
  o Large number of participant sites.
  o Regular communications between data providers and users, encouraging higher data quality.
- Network weaknesses:
  o Variable instrumentation platforms.
  o Metadata are sometimes limited.

The CWOP network is a public-private partnership with U.S. citizens and various agencies including NOAA, NASA, and various universities. There are over 4500 registered sites worldwide, with close to 3000 of these sites located in North America.

G.6. Desert Research Institute (DRI) Network

- Purpose of network: sample weather and climate in various desert and mountain locations in support of ongoing research activities at WRCC and Desert Research Institute.
- Primary management agencies: WRCC and Desert Research Institute.
- Data website: http://www.wrcc.dri.edu.
- Measured weather/climate elements:
  o Air temperature.
  o Precipitation.
  o Relative humidity and dewpoint temperature.
  o Wind speed and direction.
  o Barometric pressure.
  o Solar radiation.
- Sampling frequency: every 3 seconds.
- Reporting frequency: every 10 minutes.
- Estimated station cost: $10000, with maintenance costs of about $2000 per year.
- Network strengths:
  o High-quality data and metadata.
  o Sites are well-maintained.
  o Data are in near-real-time
- Network weaknesses:
  o Network has relatively small geographical extent (Nevada and its immediate surroundings).

The Desert Research Institute (DRI) operates this network of automated weather stations, located primarily in California and Western Nevada. Many of these stations are located in remote mountain and desert locations and provide data that are often used in support of various mountain- and desert-based environmental studies in the region.

G.7. NPS Gaseous Pollutant Monitoring Program (GPMP)

- Purpose of network: measurement of ozone and related meteorological elements.
- Primary management agency: NPS.
- Data website: http://www2.nature.nps.gov/air/monitoring.
- Measured weather/climate elements:
  - Air temperature.
  - Relative humidity.
  - Precipitation.
  - Wind speed and direction.
  - Solar radiation.
  - Surface wetness.
- Sampling frequency: continuous.
- Reporting frequency: hourly.
- Estimated station cost: unknown.
- Network strengths:
  - Stations are located within NPS park units.
  - Data quality is excellent, with high data standards.
  - Provides unique measurements that are not available elsewhere.
  - Records are up to 2 decades in length.
  - Site maintenance is excellent.
  - Thermometers are aspirated.
- Network weaknesses:
  - Not easy to download the entire data set or to ingest live data.
  - Station spacing and coverage: station installation is episodic, driven by opportunistic situations.

The NPS web site indicates that there are 33 sites with continuous ozone analysis run by NPS, with records from a few to about 16-17 years. Of these stations, 12 are labeled as GPMP sites and many of these are collocated with CASTNet sites. All of these have standard meteorological measurements, including a 10-m mast. Another nine GPMP sites are located within NPS units but run by cooperating agencies. A number of other sites (1-2 dozen) ran for differing periods in the past, generally less than 5-10 years.

G.8. National Atmospheric Deposition Program (NADP)

- Purpose of network: measurement of precipitation chemistry and atmospheric deposition.
- Primary management agencies: USDA, but multiple collaborators.
- Data website: http://nadp.sws.uiuc.edu.
- Measured weather/climate elements:
  - Precipitation.
- Sampling frequency: daily.
- Reporting frequency: daily.
- Estimated station cost: unknown.
- Network strengths:
  - Data quality is excellent, with high data standards.
  - Site maintenance is excellent.

- Network weaknesses:
  - o A very limited number of climate parameters are measured.

Stations within the NADP network monitor primarily wet deposition through precipitation chemistry at selected sites around the U.S. and its territories. The network is a collaborative effort among several agencies including USGS and USDA. Precipitation is the primary climate parameter measured at NADP sites.

G.9. USDA/NRCS Snowcourse Network (NRCS-SC)

- Purpose of network: collect snowpack and related climate data to assist in forecasting water supply in the western United States.
- Primary management agency: NRCS.
- Data website: http://www.wcc.nrcs.usda.gov/snowcourse/.
- Measured weather/climate elements:
  - o Snow depth.
  - o Snow water equivalent.
- Sampling, reporting frequency: monthly or seasonally.
- Estimated station cost: cost of man-hours needed to set up snowcourse and make measurements.
- Network strengths:
  - o Periods of record are generally long.
  - o Large number of high-altitude sites.
- Network weaknesses:
  - o Measurement and reporting only occurs on monthly to seasonal basis.
  - o Few weather/climate elements are measured.

USDA/NRCS maintains a network of snow-monitoring stations known as snowcourses. Many of these sites have been in operation since the early part of the twentieth century. These are all manual sites where only snow depth and snow water content are measured.

G.10. Portable Ozone Monitoring System (POMS)

- Purpose of network: provide seasonal, short-term (1-5 years) monitoring of near-surface atmospheric ozone levels in remote locations.
- Primary management agency: NPS.
- Data website: http://www2.nature.nps.gov/air/studies/portO3.htm.
- Measured weather/climate elements:
  - o Air temperature.
  - o Precipitation.
  - o Relative humidity.
  - o Wind speed and direction.
  - o Solar radiation.
- Sampling frequency: hourly.
- Reporting frequency: hourly.
- Estimated station cost: $20000 with operation and maintenance costs of up to $10000/year.
- Network strengths:

o High-quality data.

o Site maintenancc is excellent.

- Network weaknesses:

o No long-term sites, so not as useful for climate monitoring.

o Sites are somewhat expensive to operate.

The POMS network is operated by the NPS Air Resources Division. Sites are intended primarily for summer, short-term (1-5 years) monitoring of near-surface atmospheric ozone levels in remote locations. Measured meteorological elements include temperature, precipitation, wind, relative humidity, and solar radiation.

G.11. Remote Automated Weather Station (RAWS) Network

- Purpose of network: provide near-real-time (hourly or near hourly) measurements of meteorological variables for use in fire weather forecasts and climatology. Data from RAWS also are used for natural resource management, flood forecasting, natural hazard management, and air-quality monitoring.
- Primary management agency: WRCC, National Interagency Fire Center.
- Data website: http://www.raws.dri.edu/index.html.
- Measured weather/climate elements:

o Air temperature.

o Precipitation.

o Relative humidity.

o Wind speed.

o Wind direction.

o Wind gust.

o Gust direction.

o Solar radiation.

o Soil moisture and temperature.

- Sampling frequency: 1 or 10 minutes, element-dependent.
- Reporting frequency: generally hourly. Some stations report every 15 or 30 minutes.
- Estimated station cost: $12000 with satellite telemetry ($8000 without satellite telemetry); maintenance costs are around $2000/year.
- Network strengths:

o Metadata records are usually complete.

o Sites are located in remote areas.

o Sites are generally well-maintained.

o Entire period of record available on-line.

- Network weaknesses:

o RAWS network is focused largely on fire management needs (formerly focused only on fire needs).

o Frozen precipitation is not measured reliably.

o Station operation is not always continuous.

o Data transmission is completed via one-way telemetry. Data are therefore recoverable either in real-time or not at all.

The RAWS network is used by many land-management agencies, such as the BLM, NPS, Fish and Wildlife Service, Bureau of Indian Affairs, Forest Service, and other agencies. The RAWS network was one of the first automated weather station networks to be installed in the United States. Most gauges do not have heaters, so hydrologic measurements are of little value when temperatures dip below freezing or reach freezing after frozen precipitation events. There are approximately 1100 real-time sites in this network and about 1800 historic sites (some are decommissioned or moved). The sites can transmit data all winter but may be in deep snow in some locations. The WRCC is the archive for this network and receives station data and metadata through a special connection to the National Interagency Fire Center in Boise, Idaho.

G.12. NWS/FAA Surface Airways Observation (SAO) Network

- Purpose of network: provide near-real-time (hourly or near hourly) measurements of meteorological variables and are used both for airport operations and weather forecasting.
- Primary management agency: NOAA, FAA.
- Data website: data are available from state climate offices, RCCs (e.g., WRCC, http://www.wrcc.dri.edu), and NCDC (http://www.ncdc.noaa.gov).
- Measured weather/climate elements:
  o Air temperature.
  o Dewpoint and/or relative humidity.
  o Wind speed.
  o Wind direction.
  o Wind gust.
  o Gust direction.
  o Barometric pressure.
  o Precipitation (not at many FAA sites).
  o Sky cover.
  o Ceiling (cloud height).
  o Visibility.
- Sampling frequency: element-dependent.
- Reporting frequency: element-dependent.
- Estimated station cost: $100000–$200000, with maintenance costs approximately $10000/year.
- Network strengths:
  o Records generally extend over several decades.
  o Consistent maintenance and station operations.
  o Data record is reasonably complete and usually high quality.
  o Hourly or sub-hourly data.
- Network weaknesses:
  o Nearly all sites are located at airports.
  o Data quality can be related to size of airport—smaller airports tend to have poorer datasets.
  o Influences from urbanization and other land-use changes.

These stations are managed by NOAA, U. S. Navy, U. S. Air Force, and FAA. These stations are located generally at major airports and military bases. The FAA stations often do not record precipitation, or they may provide precipitation records of reduced quality. Automated stations are typically ASOSs for the NWS or AWOSs for the FAA. Some sites only report episodically with observers paid per observation.

G.13. USDA/NRCS Snowfall Telemetry (SNOTEL) network

- Purpose of network: collect snowpack and related climate data to assist in forecasting water supply in the western United States.
- Primary management agency: NRCS.
- Data website: http://www.wcc.nrcs.usda.gov/snow/.
- Measured weather/climate elements:
  - o Air temperature.
  - o Precipitation.
  - o Snow water content.
  - o Snow depth.
  - o Relative humidity (enhanced sites only).
  - o Wind speed (enhanced sites only).
  - o Wind direction (enhanced sites only).
  - o Solar radiation (enhanced sites only).
  - o Soil moisture and temperature (enhanced sites only).
- Sampling frequency: 1-minute temperature; 1-hour precipitation, snow water content, and snow depth. Less than one minute for relative humidity, wind speed and direction, solar radiation, and soil moisture and temperature (all at enhanced site configurations only).
- Reporting frequency: reporting intervals are user-selectable. Commonly used intervals are every one, two, three, or six hours.
- Estimated station cost: $20000 with maintenance costs approximately $2000/year.
- Network strengths:
  - o Sites are located in high-altitude areas that typically do not have other weather or climate stations.
  - o Data are of high quality and are largely complete.
  - o Very reliable automated system.
- Network weaknesses:
  - o Historically limited number of elements.
  - o Remote so data gaps can be long.
  - o Metadata sparse and not high quality; site histories are lacking.
  - o Measurement and reporting frequencies vary.
  - o Many hundreds of mountain ranges still not sampled.
  - o Earliest stations were installed in the late 1970s; temperatures have only been recorded since the 1980s.

USDA/NRCS maintains a set of automated snow-monitoring stations known as the SNOTEL (snowfall telemetry) network. These stations are designed specifically for cold and snowy locations. Precipitation and snow water content measurements are intended for hydrologic applications and water-supply forecasting, so these measurements are measured generally to within 2.5 mm (0.1 in.). Snow depth is tracked to the nearest 25 mm, or one inch. These stations function year around.

G.14. University of California Santa Barbara (UCSB) Network

- Purpose of network: provide weather data in support of environmental science research projects, primarily in SEKI.
- Data website: unavailable.
- Measured weather/climate elements:
  o Air temperature.
  o Relative humidity.
  o Precipitation.
  o Wind speed and direction.
  o Wind gust and direction.
  o Solar Radiation.
- Sampling frequency: unknown.
- Reporting frequency: unknown.
- Estimated station cost: unknown.
- Network strengths:
  o Stations located in remote areas, such as the upper Marble Fork of the Kaweah.
- Network weaknesses:
  o Station maintenance and data quality are uncertain.
  o Station coverage is limited.

These stations are maintained and operated by UCSB's Donald Bren School of Environmental Science and Management. This department runs several research projects, primarily in SEKI.

G.15. Weather For You Network (WX4U)

- Purpose of network: allow volunteer weather enthusiasts around the U.S. to observe and share weather data.
- Data website: http://www.met.utah.edu/jhorel/html/mesonet.
- Measured weather/climate elements:
  o Air temperature.
  o Relative humidity and dewpoint temperature.
  o Precipitation.
  o Wind speed and direction.
  o Wind gust and direction.
- Sampling frequency: 10 minutes.
- Reporting frequency: 10 minutes.
- Estimated station cost: unknown.
- Network strengths:
  o Stations are located throughout the U.S.
  o Stations provide near-real-time observations.
- Network weaknesses:
  o Instrumentation platforms can be variable.
  o Data are sometimes of questionable quality.

The WX4U network is a nationwide collection of weather stations run by local observers. Meteorological elements that are measured usually include temperature, precipitation, wind, and humidity.

Appendix H. Additional weather and climate stations

Name	Lat.	Lon.	Elev. (m)	Network	Start	End
Atwell	36.467	-118.667	1975	USACE	1949	1984
Bear Hill	36.567	-118.767	2025	USACE	1966	1984
Beartrap Meadow	36.683	-118.867	2075	USACE	1966	1984
Hockett Meadow	36.367	-118.650	2590	USACE	1965	1984
Beach Meadows	36.127	-118.293	2332	CSS	1982	Present
Black Springs	38.375	-120.192	1981	CSS	1976	Present
Bloods Creek	38.450	-120.033	2195	CSS	1976	Present
Casa Vieja Meadows	36.200	-118.268	2530	CSS	1987	Present
Leavitt Lake	38.282	-119.622	2926	CSS	1989	Present
Leavitt Meadows	38.305	-119.552	2195	CSS	1980	Present
Lobdell Lake	38.440	-119.377	2804	CSS	1976	Present
Pascoes	35.967	-118.350	2789	CSS	1971	Present
Sonora Pass Bridge	38.318	-119.602	2667	CSS	1967	Present
Virginia Lakes Ridge	38.077	-119.233	2835	CSS	1967	Present

NPS/SIEN/NRTR—2007/042, June 2007

www.ingramcontent.com/pod-product-compliance
Lightning Source LLC
Chambersburg PA
CBHW081111290526
45795CB00006B/2084